40 Days TO Freedom

40 Days to Freedom

TO
Freedom

Live the Miracle!

Tom Lomas

freedom
ministries, inc.

Published by:
Freedom Ministries, Inc.
1855 W. State Road 434, Suite 250
Longwood, FL 32750-5071

To order additional copies or to contact Tom Lomas
write to the publisher.

Dedication

Thanks to Tom W. for his friendship and encouragement; to Jimmy for his love strategy; to Ike for his very constrictive criticism; to the inmates of Lake Correctional and Tamoka Correctional Institutions for their faith, hope and love; to Kairos team member brothers and sisters for their encouragement and for living His command; to Phyllis for her catching enthusiasm and dedication; to Blair and Big Al for proving the miracle is transferable; to daughter Chris for her generosity and sharing her artistic talent; and to daughter Peggy for her endless assistance and wisdom.

Contents

FORTY DAYS TO FREEDOM

FOREWORD

It all started with a game of golf. It was one of those particularly abysmal rounds of golf that lead to lunch and commiseration at the 19th hole, better known to those not afflicted with the mental disorder of enjoying golf as the snack bar. My golfing buddy for the day was a kindred spirit I had met, where else, playing golf. One topic of conversation turned to another until my friend was talking about a book he had written called *Forty Days to Freedom*. The heretofore anonymous golfer I am talking about is Tom Lomas, whose book you are about to read.

Tom proceeded to tell me about the lifelong addiction that he had and how he had been led to embark on the first *Forty Days to Freedom* journey, its healing results and his ensuing inspiration to write this book. Although a skeptic by nature, I was impressed with Tom's ease and openness as he unfolded his story. I was also dumbfounded because of the fact that I had dealt with (make that repressed) the same addiction myself for most of my life. The more he talked, the more I wanted to experience my own forty days to freedom. So, on the way home, we stopped at this office and Tom gave me a draft copy of *Forty Days to Freedom*. Thus armed, I began my own forty day journey the next morning.

After finishing my first day's reading, meditation and prayer, which, incidentally, takes only a couple of minutes, I wondered if at some point down the line there would be a profusion of light streaming though my window or the sound of cosmic trumpets announcing that I had been miraculously changed and that the load that I had been carrying had been lifted from my shoulders or, conversely, would this work at all?

What *did* happen was none of the above! Rather, the process for me as like that of an athlete in training. The first day's workout does not prepare him of her to run the race or play the game.

However, by working out diligently each day, a time will come when that athlete will know he or she is ready. That was my experience. Somewhere along about the twenty-fifth day or so, I began to feel a little different. Things that used to get my attention no longer did, and upon a little reflection it became obvious why. I was using the same process that Jesus used. After being baptized by John, He went off into the desert to fast and to pray for forty days to conform Himself to the will and understanding of the Father. Because of that He was able to resist the temptations of the world as offered by the adversary and preform His earthly ministry. No wonder I was getting some results! I was also doing what Paul taught in his letter to the Romans in chapter twelve verse two,

> Do not conform any longer to the pattern of this work, but be transformed by the renewing of your mind. They you will be able to rest and approve what God's will is — his good, pleasing and perfect will. (NIV)

So what can *Forty Days to Freedom* do for you? That, I would say, is mostly up to you. It gave me insight and peace. *Forty Days to Freedom* is like anything else that is successful in this life; it is a process. It is not a quick fix. It is a wonderful vehicle for transformation. The transforming agent is the unconditional love for God that is always flowing out of us. What each of us must release is the attachment of our ego and the passing pleasures and lures for the physical world. We must no longer be conformed to the world or our old ways of doing things.

No matter what you seek from *Forty Days to Freedom*, whether it's a release from an addiction or a great way to renew your mind and spirit at the beginning of a new year, I heartily recommend the investment of your time and effort. May you find all that you seek as you begin your *Forty Days to Freedom*.

Blair Steelman

Foreword

Chapter 1

JOURNEY TO A NEW BEGINNING

This message is for those of us who are hopeless and desperate and out of control, and for those who think they're in control yet are unhappy or not fulfilled, and for those wonderfully happy people who realize they still have room for growth, improvement and fulfillment. Does someone or something else control my mind, my thoughts? Oh, not all the time, I rationalize. But if I'm honest with myself for just a minute, I realize my problem affects every aspect of my life - my relationships with others, my work, my spiritual life, my success in life. I realize I am not in control of my life.

Suppose I'm not out of control; I don't have a monster within. I'm a normal, happy person. This message isn't for me, right? Wrong! My normal situation does put me at a disadvantage since desperation and open-mindedness so often go hand-in-hand. I may see what is presented here as a challenge to my status-quo. But if I am truly a happy person, nothing here will threaten me. Instead it will only add to that happiness and I can anticipate greater fulfillment. But if my happiness is shallow, comes in flashes, doesn't last, if I am incomplete, there is a great challenge here — the challenge to discover true, lasting happiness that can never be taken from me. This lasting happiness can only be attained by fulfilling the purpose for my humanity. The keys to a happy, successful life through self-control and personal fulfillment will be presented in these pages.

Before I go any further, let me air one point critical to benefiting from this writing. I should also add that this reading may be for the benefit of someone you know, perhaps someone close to you, a friend or a family member. The point we must establish is self-honesty. We must be absolutely honest with ourselves. Why would I stress this? So often people with deep-rooted, obsessive problems blame their misfortunes on other people or circumstances or bad luck — anything but themselves.

You see, if I am to purge myself of this problem, I must first admit to myself that the problem is within me. The problem is not me; it is within me. The problem is despicable, disgusting, ugly. I am beautiful, loved (more on this later), a masterpiece. I cannot be other. Again, the problem is within me; I have it. It may be very deeply entrenched but the problem is not me.

This self-honesty also includes believing we are curable. No matter how we have been indoctrinated in the past, we are curable. No matter what our obsession, bad habit, perversion, insanity, or demon, if we can comprehend the written word, we are curable. To believe otherwise is a cop-out, a surrender to our worst enemy. How can this be true? We will invoke the greatest power in the universe. Nothing can withstand it. But first we must be honest with ourselves.

Have you ever noticed that when people are introduced, after the name, the occupation is the most desired information about the person? What does a person's occupation or profession really tell us about that person? Not a whole lot. It may give us some insight into their financial status or, perhaps, interests, although a lot of people hate their occupations and may have their main interests outside of their livelihoods. The real person will not be revealed simply by occupation. The real person will be revealed when we discover how much he or she cares for other people.

The same can be said for external appearance. We may see beauty on the outside but this may be a mask for what lies within, the real person. People are very good at masking and keeping their true selves a secret. Are we such people? Could I be afraid to reveal the true me? Do I pretend to be someone I am not? Am I ashamed of the real me beneath the facade?

If I am ashamed, I need to listen carefully. *The me beneath the facade is not me!* Each of us is a masterpiece, a unique creation of the master Creator, something to feel good about. If I don't feel good about me, it's because someone or something is trying to enslave me to ugliness.

Another Someone still believes in us, no matter what our past. Someone wants to bring us back. Someone loves us so much He'll follow us to the depths of hell to bring us back, to nourish and heal us, and to break our chains of enslavement. He'll give us a freedom we've never known before (or perhaps it is so far in our past that we've totally forgotten). And, once set free, we'll owe no debt to our redeemer. In fact, after the gift of our freedom, He will shower many more gifts upon us if we want them. The price? Simply that we want them and agree to accept them. And these gifts are far better than anything we have ever received before. The first gift is our freedom. Are we ready to start receiving? Then let's begin.

The key to lasting happiness will be passed to us. Read this book in sequence. Don't jump ahead to find the key quickly. That won't work. This is important since we are given a plan of action that starts with a preparation followed by a challenging yet fulfilling forty-day journey. Don't worry. We won't have to get time off from work. We'll take this most amazing journey of our life during our regular daily routine. Then we'll have a post-trip briefing which will allow us to continue this wonderful journey for the rest of our life to its ultimate, glorious destination.

So, again, if we want the full benefit from this experience, read in sequence. We must make a determined, conscious effort to trust, to believe, to hope just one more time. If something within tells us "hogwash," that something must be defeated if we are to be free. We must dare to trust and be vulnerable just one last time.

Do we at times feel all alone in the world? Do we feel as if everyone is against us or that no one understands us? This is a terrible feeling but there is good news: we never have to be alone again! Someone is always with us, is always watching, is always there for us, is never against us, and always understands us. This Someone is God. He is our parent and He is our partner — that's right, our partner. He has a vested stake in our every thought and action because He wants only the best for us.

God will not manipulate us. His love for us is so complete He has given us the freedom to refuse Him. But He's always there, always waiting for our call, anxious to answer. We can call on Him whenever we need a friend. But don't expect Him to answer our call on our terms. Remember He is God and only wants what is best for us, so we must allow Him to answer on His terms. Then we can trust that the answer will always be right for us. It may not be the answer we desire since, as humans, we don't always want what is best for ourselves.

Have we ever been in partnership with someone? Perhaps a business or investment partnership comes to mind; but there are other types of partnerships, such as marriage or friendship. It's tough for partnerships of all types to survive nowadays with equality such a big issue. Do we really believe humans can ever create true equality? Too often, petty jealousies arise, where one partner feels he's doing more work than the other or feels the other partner is receiving more than his share of the rewards.

Lucky for us, our partnership with God is on a different scale. I think of God as my senior partner who has responsibility for providing me with guidance, direction, strength, motivation, ideas, persistence and much more. What's my responsibility to the partnership? To have faith in Him, faith in His existence, faith in His Word, faith in His love for me. Just imagine having a partner who wants to take more and more of our burden onto His shoulders, whereas His primary reward is our happiness.

Perhaps this has not been our experience. We haven't felt that God is our partner. Perhaps the existence of some other partner or partners has interfered with our relationship with God. The past is history. It cannot be changed so don't let it disturb us. In our hand is the key to unlock a new beginning, a new partnership, a new me. Let's give ourselves a chance.

Perhaps we have searched for freedom in religion, with psychiatrists or psychologists, by changing geography, changing careers or even changing mates. Perhaps we've even contemplated suicide, since nothing has worked and we feel so alone and empty. Oh sure, maybe a strategy seemed to work for a while; we thought we had the answer but it didn't last. I've been there. I've walked in the shoes of the person not in full control of his thoughts and actions and not in love with the person he sees in the mirror.

I am here now to state that each one of us is like a precious, beautiful pearl in God's eyes and we can be free! We can be in full control of our thoughts and actions. Risk it! Just imagine if I'm right! Totally free, totally healed, totally in control of our thoughts and actions for the first time in our life. This is the greatest gift we will ever receive. Trust just one more time. We will not fail. The method will not fail for it was invented by the One who is infallible.

After experiencing our forty days, we will be free to do anything we wish. But be forewarned: What we wish to do now and what we wish to do after attaining our freedom may be entirely different. There is a purpose for our existence, a reason for our being here. We may even be aware of it yet are unable to fulfill it. It's actually quite simple since we were all born to love one another. This is our prime directive. This is what God wants us to do in our own unique circumstance.

This love, the only real, true love, is a love of giving, not getting. It is synonymous with charity, but in a non-condescending way. But how? How do we love others? In every way we can. Be especially mindful of the special gifts or talents God has given us. They have a purpose in serving Him. If we are ready and open to their use, God will allow the opportunities for their use. But we may not be ready.

A lot has happened from our birth to now to block our lines of communication with our Creator. Our intent here is to help us remove the major obstacle to our fulfillment of the best life we can live, to help us create a new person who isn't really new but simply the real person who has been hidden from others and ourself for a long time.

True, lasting happiness is rooted in serving God by loving each other. This is the reason we are all here. This is why any happiness which comes from getting is shallow and fleeting. We are all on a quest for happiness, fulfillment and freedom. Isn't it amazing that all three are attained with the same answer? Love! Now it's time to unlock the real me, the loving me, and eliminate all that stands in the way of our true happiness and fulfillment in life.

My Lord, look on Your creation and have pity. Open my mind, my eyes, my ears, my heart, and let me receive Your healing counsel. I know that You are the source of all that is good and beautiful; yet I have closed my heart to You. I pray that You will remove all obstacles between us that I may come to know and serve You again. For to know and serve You is to find the everlasting peace and happiness and fulfillment for which my soul yearns.

Chapter 2

WHAT ABOUT OUR BAGGAGE?

Are we feeling forsaken, as if God has forgotten us? Have we asked for His help, really asked? This is important, because sometimes our affliction can become a crutch we're unwilling to give up. It becomes an excuse for suffering; and, as ridiculous as it may seem, we may be reluctant to change. We must come to the point where, no matter what, we are ready for change, ready to grow up, because that's exactly what's happening — we're growing up.

Sometimes growing up can be scary. It can eliminate our excuse for failure. Take heart! It's worth it! God has allowed our affliction for a purpose. Everything that happens, the good and the bad, He allows to happen for a purpose. He may be tempering us for the task ahead. What task? Our creation, too, was for a purpose, but we can't fulfill our purpose while we're dancing with Satan. We can't serve two masters. We must be cleansed of our corruption before we're ready to serve God. If not, we'll find ourselves leading a Jekyll-Hyde existence. We may perform worthy tasks for God but our plague will always come back.

God has not forsaken us. He allowed His own Son to die an agonizing death nailed to a cross, but it was for a purpose. He did not forsake Him. Jesus paid the greatest price to serve His Father, but it was for a purpose. Hanging on that wooden cross, He took all the sins of all the people of the world — past, present and future — and paid the ultimate price for them with His life. His was the ultimate purpose, opening the gates of heaven for all of us.

Jesus also received the ultimate reward for fulfilling His purpose, the same reward that He now makes possible for all of us: a life of eternal bliss with His Father, our Father.

Our purpose may not be of the magnitude of Jesus', but it is important to God; therefore, it should be important to us. In order to fulfill God's purpose for our existence, we must be ready for the task ahead. We are not ready if Satan owns us, but we can break our bondage if we truly want to. God will not force us to fulfill our purpose on earth. We must make a voluntary decision to serve God in a unique service, unique to us. This must become more important to us than our sin. When we are ready to make the sacrifice to give up our sin, to commit to God's way, we are ready for our forty days of cleansing.

How do we spend most of our time? When we're young, we spend a lot of time preparing for when we're adults. Studies, school, sports and work comprise most of our time. Most of our studies involve preparing us for careers and for management of our future lives — our physical lives. But how much time do we spend in preparation for our eternal lives?

Studies, school, sports and work are all good, but they are not really important on their own. Their importance lies in their use as tools to achieve results. Certainly the results include survival of the human species on earth, and today we're learning that we can't just continue taking from Mother Nature without giving back. The same is true of our human relations. If during our lifetimes we continuously take from others without regard to their well-being, we are seeing to our own spiritual extinction.

Our lives are filled with opportunities to serve others during our studies, during our time in school and sports activities, and in our work and leisure time. We are constantly making contact with other people. Do we see these contacts as opportunities for exploitation or for service? They can always be opportunities for service, which is a synonym for love.

None of our day-to-day contacts is by accident. Everything that happens in our life is allowed to happen for a reason. Every contact with another human being is an opportunity for service, an opportunity for love, an opportunity for us to learn about life, an opportunity for us to learn about ourselves.

Let's suppose for a minute, upon reflection about our past human contact opportunities, we assess that we did more taking than giving. If we were to consider our past experiences a test, we flunked! But let's also imagine our teacher is a benevolent, forgiving person who is willing to wipe the slate clean starting right now and won't hold our past errors against us. Would that be hoping for too much?

This, my friend, is exactly the opportunity we now hold in our hands, the opportunity to change into the wonderful person we were created to be. In fact, we are already that person right now. The fact that we are reading this demonstrates our desire for a new start. All that remains to effect our transformation to the real person is to throw out the garbage and make room for the good stuff.

When we pass from this life to eternity, we'll be allowed no baggage, not one earthly possession. Why then do we place so much importance on getting things in this life instead of building treasure in heaven? The more we love, the closer we are to God, the more Godlike we are and the more perfect our union with Him in eternity and on earth. But our baggage interferes with this process. It competes with God for our attention, our dedication, our love. That's right! We love our baggage, yet we can't take one item of it with us.

This baggage consists not only of our material possessions but of everything that interferes with our pursuing God's prime directive, which is simply to love our fellow human beings. Therefore, sin, too, becomes our baggage, demands our time and attention and enslaves us. And, if it becomes too powerful, society condones it as okay. Modern-day examples are materialism, promiscuity, abortion and perversion, to name a few. We may disguise and condone these as love, but when put to the test, we find them to be a love of greed and lust, which is foreign to the charitable love of God. The results of the test are frustration, dissatisfaction, lack of peace and alienation from God. Yet we persist in our misguided ways. We demand our rights. We demand justice. Foolish children! We can never find equal rights among men. Human society will never be just, so our efforts are misdirected. We must stop valuing equality, justice and freedom in the perverted eyes of men and instead seek them through the eyes of God, for only in His way are they attainable.

Bond to God. Elevate your goals from mortal attainments to the one goal of pleasing God. Instead of focusing on all the things we don't have, praise God for all the wondrous gifts He has given us. Practice His way of charitable love to all, and we'll gain a new perspective of what is truly important and fulfilling.

Know that God is the source of all love and without God there is no love. All else that calls itself love, but denies God, is false. Misguided, false love is of Satan and is used by him to possess us. It is true that Satan wants to own our souls, and false love is one of the tricks he uses to achieve his ends. The most apparent false love is lust, not only lust for sex but also lust for material wealth and for power.

Lust for material wealth is most apparent here in the United States where both parents in families commonly have full-time jobs. This trend began for the purpose of earning extra money so the family could enjoy more luxuries. But with time an unhealthy spiral has occurred. Society has adapted to the two-income family to the extent that both incomes are now necessary to maintain a basic life-style. And what's the payoff? Do the bigger homes and nicer cars create happiness? If our answer is yes, we don't know true happiness — the happiness from seeing God in the smile of a child, in a sunset or in the uniqueness of a leaf.

Lust for power often replaces lust for wealth when the individual realizes that his greed can't be satisfied by wealth. So he thinks his happiness and fulfillment will be achieved through the possession of power over people — the ability to dominate others. Make no mistake, power used in God's service to spread His love can be a wonderful, rewarding thing, but power used to dominate or enslave others is of Satan. Through it we turn not only ourselves but others away from God, and we condemn ourselves to an eternity of horror where we reap what we have sown.

Lust for sex can fill one's mind to the exclusion of God. It can enslave the soul and become our reason for being. It can cause us to believe the greatest worth of the opposite gender is to fulfill our own greedy physical desires. Through this powerful weapon of evil we can condemn ourselves to misery and depravity for all eternity. Be very clear on this: We condemn ourselves. It is our choice. How foolish this false love, this false happiness, this false gratification! How foolish when we choose this misleading way of life for the brief time we're here on earth and thereby condemn our souls to hell for all eternity. How foolish, when any gratification of sexual lust pales in comparison to the ecstasy of being filled with the Holy Spirit. Don't misunderstand. When physical love grows out of true love — God's love — it is not only good and fulfilling, but it is God's gift to us. This is a unique gift through which He bonds man and woman to each other and to Him by creating another trinity: God, man and woman. And, just as with the blessed trinity of Father, Son and Holy Spirit, the three become one.

Through our love for God we gain the strength to overcome the human passions that will destroy us. At the same time we ignite the passions that will grant us bliss for all eternity. By overcoming our greed for flesh and money and power, we are set free, truly free, to lust for God and all He offers. We experience the understanding of gaining by giving. Suddenly the personal ambitions of our old, greedy lives pale in importance and are replaced by a new dedication, a new strength, a new experience of joy and peace and fulfillment which can only be attained by surrender to God and His way.

My God, I have lusted for the wrong things. Cure my blindness that I may see with new eyes the path to everlasting bliss with You. Give me the courage to break all bonds with Satan so I may be free to choose You.

What About Our Baggage?

Chapter 3

WHERE ARE WE GOING?

What is freedom? We all want to be free but do we fully understand what we are after? Does it mean the ability to do whatever we want, or is freedom a state of mind and spirit? Can we be free even if we are in prison? Can freedom exist without happiness? What is happiness and how can we achieve it?

If we are to believe in God, then we must

understand our final goal as humans, which is heaven. Heaven is not a place but a state of being. The closest we can come to describing it with our limited human vocabulary is bliss. When we are in heaven, we have come home to our Father. We are united with Him for all eternity. He is our home. He is our final resting place.

This all happens when our mortal bodies die and we, our spirits, are released from their physical confines. But this only occurs if we have made the choice of heaven during our mortal lives. This is why we are here. This is why we are born — to make this free choice. This is the ultimate freedom that no one can take from us, no matter where we are born, no matter what our circumstances. Thus we are created free by the greatest power in the universe, God Himself, who refuses to enslave us. Just think about that for a minute. He loves and respects us so much that He refuses to enslave us.

Others will try to take away our freedom and, when we come right down to it, what they're trying to take is our freedom to choose God and His way. You see, it all boils down to good over evil. These others are not just the evil rulers we've seen through history. They consist of Satan and his lieutenants. Who are Satan's lieutenants? Anyone who would sway us from God. These are not always evil people, but they are being used for evil purposes. They may be well-intentioned, even generous, but they are being used, often without their own realization, to divert us from God. And such an attempt to divert, no matter how innocent, is evil at work because it is an attempt to steal our only real chance for freedom, which is with God. These lieutenants of Satan may be found in our workplace, among our friends, in our families, even in ourselves in our influence over others.

So what do we do about this? Do we shun these people? Do we crawl into a hole of isolation? To the contrary, we become lieutenants of God working to influence ourselves and others to God's way. If we're successful, we are setting souls free, minds free to experience the greatest freedom that exists: freedom of mind, freedom of spirit.

Instead of trying to enslave through lies and deceit, God tries to persuade us to follow Him. How? By giving Himself to us in the form of Jesus. Jesus set the example for our lives as humans. If we accept and live His example, then we have made the choice for God's way. Heaven becomes our ultimate goal, our ultimate happiness. However, we must live His example, not for the attainment of heaven, but for the example itself — love. And love is only love if it is given unselfishly without hope for personal reward.

Jesus is love incarnate, love made man. His whole life on earth was one of love for us, a life of constant giving: giving in His healing of the sick, giving in casting out demons, giving in teaching us about God, giving in revealing Himself as the Son of the Father, giving in His compassion for all those in need, giving in His ultimate sacrifice upon the cross. This was His choice to show us the way our Father wants us to live. This is the way to the happiness we all seek, not only the happiness of the bliss of heaven but the true happiness we can experience during our mortal lives. If we live His way, if we really try to follow His example, He rewards us now with a taste of heaven, a preview of what is to come. Peter, with great wisdom and insight, told Jesus that He had "the words of everlasting life." If we read the words spoken by Christ we, like Peter, will also find "the words of everlasting life."

His words are the one truth on which we can totally rely. He is the one Person of history who never lied. This is why His apostles followed Him; they knew He spoke only the truth; they came to know Him as the source of all truth. He is the only Person who will never let us down and never lie to us.

The only way to find the ultimate truth and the reason for our creation is through studying the words He spoke as recorded in the four Gospels of the New Testament. These words, actually spoken by God Himself in the flesh, are the keys which open the gates of heaven to us. If we read them with a clear, open, thirsting mind, we'll discover, as Peter, "the words of eternal life" (John 6:68).

Jesus gave us a personal goal of achieving perfection. This is possible through our love. God is love, and we achieve perfection in His eyes by loving perfectly as He loves us. This is a love of giving, not getting. This is how we follow Jesus. What do we give? Ourselves. And by giving ourselves unselfishly, by giving our love, we give

God. To whom? To everyone! Not just to our neighbor who is easy to love, but to the one who is impossible to love — the sinner, the outcast from society, the criminal, the depraved. Since God loves these as much as He loves us, we have no right to withhold our love from them.

If our love is rejected, it's not our problem. As long as we give, we have done our part. We might be just one step on the way back to God for someone who became lost; or we might be the first step for someone who has never known God. For many, we may be their only chance to be set free from the chains of sin and attain the perfection their heavenly Father desires.

This becomes natural, the opposite of a hoarded treasure. This is a treasure which must be given, because by giving we receive a taste of the happiness God has waiting for us after our mortal lives end. This is the opposite of what society teaches: hoard, win, conquer, rule, get all you can. Answer this: Are people who play by society's rules and standards ever truly happy, content or at peace? Are they free? Or are they enslaved by their greed? What if God does exist? What if we did play by His rules? What do we really have to lose? Only the emptiness and dissatisfaction that comes from our greed. But if He's real, and if He's really telling the truth in His written Word, the Bible, what do we have to gain? Eternal bliss! Just imagine! Eternity is a long time. In comparison, our mortal lives are merely the wink of an eye. If, by living by His rules, we're happy and content and at peace and have a shot at eternal bliss, doesn't that beat any of the alternatives? Why not try? Think about it. We truly have nothing to lose.

To approach perfection, love must be practiced with a spirit of humility. We must surrender any feeling or attitude of superiority over others, realizing that we are all children of God.

I once heard a concept expressed that those who have tougher lives here on earth have better lives in eternity than those of us who have it easier on earth. This made sense to me and perhaps helped me to understand why God allows seemingly innocent people to suffer injustice. Perhaps another reason is to create opportunities for those of us who are more fortunate to correct and overcome injustice. If we are truly striving to become people of God, isn't this necessary? Shouldn't we share our bounty with others with a spirit of true charity and true humility?

When God decided to become human, He chose humble parents and a humble status for Himself. He walked this earth as a humble Person always serving others even to the extent of washing the feet of His apostles. He also allowed His feet to be washed to allow the expression of and the acceptance of love. Allowing others to love us and accepting their expressions of love, again with true humility on our part, is also very important.

Jesus's final act of humility was dying an agonizing death on the cross as a human, as one of us, as our brother. Even before the nails invaded

His flesh, He allowed Himself to be ridiculed, flogged, spat upon and crowned with thorns. Why did He allow this? We know, from His earlier experiences, that He was able to escape danger at will. Was this God's ultimate expression of love for His children gone astray, an ultimate demonstration of sacrifice and charity and humility, still thinking of others as He hung near death, opening the doors of paradise to the lowly thief hanging beside Him?

He gave so much for us. How can we refuse to follow His lead? When He gave us everything He had, how can we refuse to share what He has given us with our less fortunate brothers and sisters? As He told us, whatever we do for or against our fellow humans, we do for or against Him. It's our choice. Do we drive the nails deeper or do we give others, with His love, comfort and rest and dignity and justice?

Life becomes beautiful when we're walking with God. We focus more on what we have than what we lack. We become aware that everything we have is a gift from God — even something as simple as the air we breathe. It's as if we're seeing the world through different eyes. When we see suffering, we are more saddened; we are more drawn to involvement. When we see happiness and beauty, we become overwhelmed with God's creation and we wonder how people can doubt His existence.

But many don't see through our eyes. That's the greatest injustice. They can't see what we see.

They are blinded by many things and herein lies our greatest challenge: to give them our eyes, to help them see what we see. And this we will do because our greatest gift from God demands to be shared. The happiness we feel from His overflowing love cannot be contained. We must pass it on, and so we will. Perhaps we can't understand all this right now, but we will. God will help us if we just try to remain open to Him until we have experienced everything this book has to offer. He'll take care of us on our journey.

Dear God, it is so difficult for me to trust and have faith. My trust and faith have been misdirected in the past. Lord, I ask that You give me a strong faith in You so that I may realize You are the One for all my trust.

Where Are We Going?

Chapter 4

CHANGE PARTNERS

Jesus told us His kingdom is not of this world. Satan rules this world. Now many would say there is no such thing or being. Many of these same people might profess that it doesn't matter how we live our lives on earth; we'll go on to a better place. That very thought is Satan at work. Every time we underestimate him or refuse to believe that he exists, he smiles; and he's that much closer to owning us. Just as we know God exists, we know Satan exists because evil exists. Just as God is love, Satan is evil. He not only exists, but Jesus told us the world is his kingdom. Therefore, if we are to attain true freedom, true happiness, true fulfillment, we must not be of this world. In other words, we must not just go along with the norm that is accepted by society. We must not accept society's rationalizations which lead to the imprisonment of our soul. We must be in the world but not of the world until the world is ruled by God, which will happen when enough of us have worked to break the bonds of Satan.

We ask, "Why doesn't God just eradicate Satan from the face of the earth if He really loves us?" That should be easy for God. His love for us is precisely the reason why God allows Satan to exist and to tempt us. Think about this: If only love and kindness and charity and goodness existed, how could we choose God? There would be no choice, no freedom. We would be little more than robots. We are men and women made in the image of God. Just look at Jesus, fully man and fully God. We are, in all of His creation, the beings who are most like Him. He loves us too much to make us slaves or robots. What He has in mind for us is a new level of relationship which we will not fully understand until we are there with Him, one with Him. But trust is required, faith is required and love is required. There is no room for any alternative to love in His heaven.

Most of us want to do something special with

our lives. We wish to create a legacy for which we'll be remembered. This is really a way we're attempting to achieve immortality. Perhaps we're caught up in this because we're not really sure what lies beyond the grave so we try to create a little insurance that at least a thought about us will live on. Here again we are being concerned with this world. Jesus told one of the men being crucified with Him that he would be in paradise with Jesus that same day. He did not say that a thought about the criminal would continue beyond his death. Instead He said that the person would be in paradise after his body breathed its last breath. If you were that man with Jesus, which would you prefer—a thought about you lingering on this earth or being in heaven with Jesus? Two thousand years later, that man is still with Jesus in His kingdom, and he will still be with him two million years from now in eternal bliss.

When we buy a computer, the machine comes with an operating system and some basic software to give us a start with our initial use. With time and need we will add software and build upon the information we gather and store in our computer. Likewise, as humans, we come into this world with a functioning body and some basic, initial knowledge. Our starting knowledge or stored instinct includes an awareness of God and a sense of what is right versus what is wrong. As we progress through childhood, information is added. But, unlike the computer, where there is a continuous building and enhancement of information and application, sometimes the information we add as humans tends to bury our initial knowledge of God and causes us to forget or reject it.

"Garbage in, garbage out" is an old saying in the computer industry. The same is true with the human machine — and we're being fed more garbage today than ever before. I'm referring to the garbage we feed our minds. It starts in childhood and continues and only worsens during adulthood.

The input comes from the news media, the entertainment industry and the people in our environment. The message is that increasing sexual freedom is OK, that violence is a way to suppress those who are against us and that materialism and power lead to self-fulfillment. As a result, we lead lives of frustration, thinking that if we get more and more, someday we'll be happy. But we never are as long as we persist in our greed. Many of us die unhappy, feeling we've missed something in life, and we have. Yet, in spite of all the mental garbage we consume over our lifetimes, our basic awareness of God will often override the garbage as we attempt to come back to Him.

This is not the way it should be. We're not created as precious reflections of God only to lose Him while growing up and then come back to Him when we're middle-aged or beyond. What a waste! We are born to reflect Him throughout our lives in a growing, improving way. We're supposed to build upon that starting software, not try to destroy it. As parents, if we are not constantly striving to instill good in our children and knowledge of their Creator, we're failing. The garbage is always there. We can't always protect our children from being exposed to it; therefore, we must attempt to offset it with what is good and healthy for their minds as well as their bodies.

Is our computer malfunctioning? Perhaps something has been missing from our operating software. Correcting the problem is not an impossible task. It can be accomplished with the addition of one command, "Love one another" (John 13:34). This was the final command given by Jesus to His apostles and, at the same time, given to all the people of the world, forever, as their basic operating system. All contacts with other people are to be expressions of love, of giving of oneself. Love our families. Love our fellow workers. Love our neighbors.

If we reject this simple remedy, we may have some blockage or overloading in our operating system. Perhaps the time has come for an overhaul that will get rid of some of the bad software we've accumulated over the years. There is just one source for our computer virus. The sooner we realize this, the better our chance for a successful overhaul. That source is Satan. His negative influences will destroy our happiness and freedom and peace of mind.

If our malfunctioning can be attributed to a single dominant problem or hangup which is interfering with our living a life of love, tune into and learn from Jesus, who purged Himself from

Satan's influence with His forty days in the desert before starting His life's work, His ministry.

A constant battle is being waged in this world between good and evil, between God and Satan. This is apparent everywhere you turn. Nations are being victimized by their leaders, employees by their bosses, bosses by their employees, children by their parents, the environment by man and so forth. Corruption, evil and greed are spreading. But another force is also spreading throughout the world. We don't hear as much about it in the media, but it's happening quietly. Love, charity and God are also spreading.

Know that the battle between good and evil is very unfair. Satan uses every dirty trick in the book and even some beyond our imagination. Satan wants to own us. He will trick us any way he can. He'll use subtle, seemingly innocent excuses to justify his way. He'll disguise his temptations as minor faults or through the phrase "I'm only human!" Before we know it, our life is on the rocks. Our yielding to his minor temptation has grown and festered until he has us completely. Our work suffers. Our spiritual life deteriorates. Our relationships become strained.

Now for the other side of the battle. God will never force Himself on us. That's why He gave us a free will — the freedom to choose or reject Him. And, unlike Satan, He doesn't want to possess us; rather He wants us to possess Him. If we do possess Him — and He's there for the asking — we can do His work on earth much like Jesus did.

Therefore, it's not up to God to eradicate Satan; it's up to us. We must be His instruments on earth. We must educate those who lack this knowledge of God so they, too, will be able to make a free choice for their eternity. We are sons and daughters of God and, therefore, brothers and sisters to each other. We cannot profess to love God and hate our brothers and sisters. Can we claim to love them if we don't make every effort to share this wonderful knowledge with them, so that they, too, can make the free choice to unite with God in paradise?

It's as if we have two lives, our earthly life and our spiritual life. Our earthly life is limited in time but has tremendous importance, because our reactions to its challenges will determine our growth in God's eyes and ultimately our quality of life in our spiritual life. The main challenge here is to elevate the importance of the spiritual above the earthly. It may help to consider the consequences of the opposite. If we live with no thought for our spiritual life and are only concerned with our tangible life on earth, what awaits us after death? If we refuse to believe in God, is it logical to think we will spend eternity with Him after rejecting His existence?

You see, whatever your concept of life after death, it becomes less than the best if it is without God. Could this possibly be the definition of hell? Eternal life without God? Perhaps, since Satan is certainly without God by his own choosing. Isn't that what Satan wants for us also, to be without God by our own choosing? The point I'm trying to make is simply that life without God isn't really life. Anyone who hasn't experienced a close, personal relationship with God has missed life.

If we live only for this world, if we are part of the "me generation," who are we kidding? If we really think this results in happiness, we are demonstrating ignorance of the awareness of God which is born within every one of us. Only by listening to Satan and absorbing his doctrines of atheism, self-fulfillment and knowledge of everything, do we bury our spiritual instincts of wanting to be with God. We fill our minds so full of self that there's no place left for God. And, again, He'll allow us to do this. He won't force His way into our lives as Satan does. God will only enter at our invitation.

Ours is often referred to as the "information age." We thirst for information of all types, including knowledge of God. It's as if the original temptation in the Garden of Eden were happening all over again. Most of us fail to realize the most important thing in life is not knowledge. To the contrary, an obsession with knowledge can cause the loss of our souls. The path to God and a blissful eternity is not through knowledge but through love.

Through the practice of unselfish love we extend to God the invitation to enter our lives. Instead of self-fulfillment, love is self-emptying. Through love we give our lives away to others. Which others? All the others who have the need for our love. All the others we meet at the crossroads of our lives.

There is a paradox here: by emptying ourselves to others, we gain the ultimate self-fulfillment for both our earthly lives and our spiritual lives. By emptying ourselves to others, we are accepting and practicing God's way as He demonstrated to us through Jesus. Thus we invite Him to walk with us on this earth, and He invites us to walk with Him in heaven. But the paradox lies in our not waiting to attain heaven until our bodies die; for when He answers our invitation, when we empty ourselves to Him by emptying ourselves to others, He fills our emptiness with Himself to overflowing. Thus we gain the most we can possibly gain by giving the most we can give. Thus we experience heaven on earth for heaven is wherever He is.

Lord, God, Creator of all that is good, open my mind to You. Help me to see that Your way, the way of charity and peace, is the way to my fulfillment. Help me to give my life to Your other children by filling their emptiness and need. Deliver me from the daily temptations of Satan and make me aware that my home, where I belong, is with You.

Chapter 5

WE ARE FORGIVEN

If love is our prime directive, then forgiveness is a necessary step on our path through human life. We cannot love and hate at the same time, or our love is blemished and is not love. If someone commits a wrong against us, we must continue loving that person. Our example is Jesus. He forgave the people who tortured and executed Him.

Have you ever been wronged or treated unjustly by anyone? Of course you have! Justice, equality and freedom are wonderful concepts, but they are far from perfect in their administration by us humans.

Forgiveness is of God. This is why we are here: to love. This is what Jesus meant when He told us to love our enemies. There is a great mystery here and a great truism. We only have to try it once to realize the great reward, the wonderful release, the freedom experienced from forgiveness.

We will have many challenges during our lifetime. These are gifts from God. They are methods or pathways to grow. And when we grow enough, when we reach the perfection desired in God's eyes, we are ready for the ultimate harvest: our close spiritual union with God when we become one with Him. Be aware, any wrong committed against us is a challenge against our willingness to love, because when we are wronged it is so much easier to hate. And when we hate, we're kicking God out and letting Satan in to enslave us to our own hate. This is why we must let go of all hate, all resentment, all unforgiveness. We must love our enemy or we cannot love God.

How can we love our enemy? How can we forgive? Try this. Realize the enemy, like you, is a creation of God and is loved no less by God than you are. It is the person we must love, not the acts. If our adversary is acting against God and His law of love, then love the adversary and pray for his conversion to God's way. If we can try to help our enemy to find the path to God, our reward from God will be great because we will be assisting God's harvest of souls.

We cannot wait with our forgiveness until our transgressors deserve pardon or ask for it. This would put us in the role of judges, which we must not be. Judgment we must leave to God. If we love only perfect people, then what is accomplished in that? If we love someone who does wrong to others but is good to us, is this a real test of love? Making friends is not part of our prime directive; creating true lovers is. Making friends can be a form of self-gratification, while true love is always unselfish. But if we can help God to create another lover, then we are not only causing God to smile, but we are also saving a soul from condemning himself and helping him to reach eternal happiness and fulfillment. Thus we are being a true friend.

Part of our duty in this conversion of others is helping them to forgive those who have wronged them and to seek forgiveness from those they have wronged. If, like Jesus, we are a living example of forgiveness, then we make the conversion easier for those who know us.

There is risk in all of this. Forgiveness may not be accepted or granted. Our act of seeking forgiveness is what is important to God and therefore to us.

Throughout His Gospels, Jesus told us our most important activity is to love and He included loving ourselves. "Well, that's natural," you say. Everybody loves himself. Not so! Some of us hold ourselves in very low esteem. In fact, some of us, who even appear conceited outwardly, are masking an interior self-hate. Why is this? Perhaps we feel guilt over some past or present action, or a thought or hang-up. Perhaps we feel inferior to other people. Perhaps we simply feel lost and can identify no purpose for our lives.

Know this! Nothing in this universe has higher value than you. You are unique and precious in God's eyes. You can be absolutely confident in this. God longs for you, yearns for you, anxiously awaits the day when you will return to Him. You started out as His, but He had to give you your freedom so you could freely return to Him. He had to give you this freedom so your return would have meaning.

Our creation itself, the fact that we exist, is a mind-boggling act of love on God's part. It has been said that "God doesn't create junk." Only man creates junk out of God's loving creation. We do so every time we abuse His gifts to us, and His gifts are everywhere.

When we abuse ourselves, in thought or action, we are attempting to create junk. This is exactly the desire of Satan. As we junk ourselves, he smiles and we are his. Fortunately for us, God will always allow us to reverse the process. This bears repeating. God will *always* allow us to recreate ourselves, from the junk that we created with the help of Satan back into God's beauty. Thus we are reborn in God's eyes, and nothing pleases Him more than our rebirth, finding what was lost, recreating beauty out of junk (though the junk never existed in the eyes of God). This is very important. We can never sink so low that God doesn't want us back. In fact, the lower we sink, the more He wants us, the more He loves us and the greater we are aware of His love during our conversion.

How do we convert? How are we reborn? How do we erase the junk so we can see the beauty God sees in us? First, recognize that we have a problem. Second, identify the problem. Third, be repentant. Finally, ask for forgiveness.

The fact that we've read this far may seem like proof that we recognize we have a problem; however, our motivation may be obtaining information for a friend or relative. So let's explore the symptoms of an existing problem.

Are we happy, really happy? Do we feel fulfilled that we're living our life in accordance with God's directives? Do we love the person we see in the mirror? The great deceiver will try to make us blind to our problems and faults, so this self-examination is necessary. If this results in our feeling that all is not right, then we have at least determined that a problem does exist.

To identify the problem, ask how our life is not in accord with God's directive. What are we doing, through thought or action, that is against loving God, loving ourselves or loving our fellow human beings? Once identified, do we now recognize our thought or action as wrong? This is necessary, as we can't ask forgiveness for something we believe is right. This may be difficult. For example, we may hate someone and feel justified because the hated person committed a terrible wrong against us or someone we hold dear. Are we justified in our hate? Who is being harmed by our hate? The hated one or us? If Jesus could forgive His executioners, do we have a right to hold our grudge? If the hated person is a creation of the same God who created us, and if God stands ready to forgive our worst transgressions and his, are we justified in withholding our forgiveness? We achieve something very special in God's eyes when we love our enemy. This is the true test of being in accord with God's directives.

Recognize, then identify our fault as a fault. Be repentant, willing to let go of our hate because only when we are willing to reverse, are we ready for God's healing. Now we are ready to ask for God's forgiveness. And when we ask, know that He forgives us no matter what.

We start with a new slate, a new beginning. Next, we dedicate ourselves to staying close to God in every way we can, through studying His written Word, through church involvement and through exercising His will of loving His people and sharing His gifts to us with others. At the same time, especially if our old ways are habitual, we must break Satan's hold on us by entering the desert of our soul for forty days.

Lord, clear the webs of Satan's deceit from my mind. Help me to see clearly my faults in Your eyes. Give me humility that I may repent for my acts against Your creation. And teach me to forgive all others as You have forgiven me.

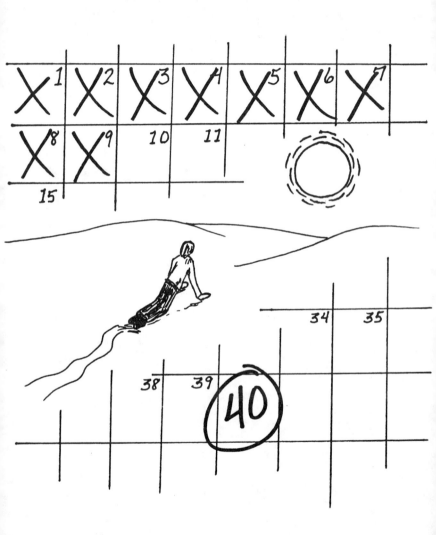

Chapter 6

FORTY DAYS IN YOUR DESERT

After His baptism in the Jordan River and before He started His ministry, Jesus went into the desert for forty days to face the temptations of Satan head-on. He also fasted during this time, perhaps to weaken Himself so His ultimate victory would be even more meaningful. It's important here that we consider the humanity of Jesus. There is evidence in the New Testament

63

that Jesus experienced human weaknesses. More than once He displayed a human temper that was most apparent when He expelled the money changers from the temple. And when He cried out from the cross, "My God, why have You forsaken Me" (Matt. 27:46), he was expressing all the pain and suffering of His agonizing death that any of us would experience in the same circumstances.

I believe this is a point too often missed by Christians. Without His humanity Jesus could not have suffered and could not have died. Many of us miss the magnitude of the great sacrifice Jesus made for humanity, for each of us. Perhaps this is why many take their Christianity so lightly. Let's face it, the "Sunday Christian" is well known. What a travesty! What a waste! Do we really think we can call ourselves Christians by putting on a holy face for an hour or two on Sunday and on Monday go back to our complacent, self-centered ways? Do we really think we're fooling God? Do we really think He is blindly going to open the gates of heaven to us after we live a farce of a life? Or perhaps, do we seal our own fate and, without even thinking about it, choose hell over heaven through our own hypocrisy?

In this modern age we ask many questions. Does hell exist? Who is it for? Does God exist? Is He loving and rewarding or angry and punishing? Does God condemn us, or do we condemn ourselves? The answers are all in the Bible. We must stop being fooled by society; the Bible, the book of life, is just as appropriate and meaningful today as when it was written. We can read the words spoken by Jesus and find for ourselves the solutions to our problems and the problems of mankind. If we have a bad habit or an addiction, we can rid ourselves of our bondage with God's help and Jesus' example. We cannot live up to our potential in any part of our life or career if we have a "plague" in our mind that interferes with our thoughts and commitments or our ability to concentrate and see things clearly.

Before He could practice the awesome commitment of fulfilling the responsibilities of the Son of God, Jesus had to clear and strengthen His mind, His will and His commitment to His Father. After His baptism in the Jordan by John the Baptist, Jesus, robed with faith and prayer, started His forty-day confrontation with weakness, temptation and evil. He used His faith in the strength His Father had given Him to survive the forty days of fasting and overcoming Satan, one day at a time, one temptation at a time. Afterward, He emerged from the desert with a mind and a will like tempered steel — and He was able to live, work and relate to others with His full potential.

In the same way, using this wonderful example of Jesus, you can purge yourself of your addictions. You can break the chains that hold you to what is against God and yourself. You can discover a new freedom, a new willpower, a new clearness of mind that you never knew existed. This is possible for each of us. This will happen for us if we truly want it to happen and if we have faith that God has given each of us the strength to overcome all evil in our lives.

Are you now at the point where you know something is wrong with your life? Has some hang-up or bad habit that may have seemed minor in the beginning taken control of your mind and your actions? Maybe you know people with willpower and you're envious. You see them as rocks! Maybe they are; but you can't really know what's going on inside them. They might be worse off than you are. A top psychologist reported that fifty percent of all men have sexual hang-ups. Another stated that all men think about sex all the time. What a sad indictment of our society. I'm here to give you the message that this is not the norm for which we were created. God created us to be good to each other in thought and action and to be happy in our union with Him for all eternity. That's right! Forever!

It's time to take the long-term perspective — longer than we'd take for financial, estate or environmental planning. What's at stake here is not financial success, passing material wealth to heirs or the air we breathe. It all pales in importance when we're dealing with the quality of life of our souls, which live not for a few years but for eternity.

We are not merely flesh and bones, blood and guts, brains and nerves and cells as perceived by science. This body that we occupy during our short existence on earth is simply a wonderful gift from God to serve us temporarily. We also are what science can't see. We are spirit, sometimes referred to as soul. Think about this. We know this is the truth. We need no proof, no evidence. Something inside, an awareness, tells us this is the truth. That something inside is the real person, the person that exists to be united with God for eternity. And in every one of us, our soul, our spirit will be restless and dissatisfied until we are home, reunited with our Creator.

Perhaps you accept this. Perhaps you have a strong faith and desire to be a good person, but there's a controlling force inside you, a force that controls your mind, a force that causes you to commit acts against your will, a force that causes you to be two people, one good, one evil. Perhaps you've prayed for healing from God to free you from your affliction, your sin, your habit, your perversion. Perhaps you have experienced temporary relief from your enslavement only to slip again in a slight moment of weakness back into the dominance of this evil force. Perhaps you've tried everything and have given up; you've decided to live as best as you can with your problem. Perhaps society is helping you by accepting your problem as normal behavior, saying it's not really a sin, saying it's just a part of being human, saying "it" has rights. But the real person, your soul, won't let you accept society's rationalizations, won't allow you peace. "Why me?" you ask. "Why has God done this to me?" You're lost! You've given up. There's no way out. People with like problems or afflictions condone it.

You accept it. Nothing more can be done. You're incurable. You quit. You are owned!

You want to be a good person. You want to attain union with God for all eternity, but you have this problem. You're only human — that's your cop-out! Your path to heaven starts by realizing that the socially acceptable mind is ruled by Satan, the originator of evil, the prince of hell. There I go again! Society says this concept of hell or eternal punishment or eternal pain doesn't exist. What if it does? What do we lose by preparing for heaven? We lose sin, guilt, unhappiness and all the empty rewards from achieving society's goals. Down deep inside, in our inner selves, in our souls, in the part of us that is immortal, we know this to be true, but something prevents us from living it. Something says that being a "goody-goody" is laughed at by society. Something says that to be acceptable by society we must be human, which is to be imperfect, which means being a little evil is OK. Thus, we give Satan, who is the embodiment of evil, the toehold he needs to eventually dominate us and rule society. Then, he very deceptively gains control of the common mind, which is society. And it all starts with just a little evil, which equates to allowing a little bit of Satan into our souls — and we really think he'll be satisfied with occupying just a little space in our lives. This is how the great deceiver wins the world.

Never quit! You can be cured! God allowed your affliction for a reason, but the reason is not your eternal damnation. If you have faith in the greatest power in the universe, you can be set free in forty days. The freedom you will experience will create a new person, the real you. This is the greatest freedom, the freedom to control your own mind, to think clearly, to be able to take on any task with total concentration, without any influence from your past affliction. The method is simple. Don't let that dissuade you. This wonderfully simple method for defeating Satan is in the life of Jesus.

You've tried running from your problem. You've tried blocking it out. You've tried rationalizing that you don't have a problem. You've tried substituting something else in your mind, maybe even something good, but your problem always comes back, doesn't it?

Now you will face your problem, your affliction, your perversion, your obsession, your demon, eye-to-eye and tell it to get lost! Before starting your forty days to freedom, you must prepare as Jesus prepared with His baptism. You must believe that God has given you the strength to overcome your problem. You must realize your value, that you deserve to succeed, that you are a unique creation of God, and He wants you healed, whole and sharing eternal happiness with Him. Now is the time to invite God to enter your soul. He wants to enter and wants you to possess Him, but He will never force Himself on you. You must choose to invite Him. When you do invite Him, He will enter. He will not refuse you! NOW is the time!

Now you have the strength you need. Now you'll start your forty days in the desert, where you will confront Satan face-to-face. You don't have to physically go into a desert, and you won't change your daily routine with your work or your family and friends. The geography isn't important; the condition of your mind is, however, as you go into the barren, parched part of your inner being, the "desert" of your soul. Here you will challenge your greatest problem, your addiction, your ruling evil force, your demon, Satan himself, who has enslaved you, and day-by-day for forty days, you will emulate Jesus. You will say, "No!" At the same time, for each of the forty days you will fortify yourself by actively seeking God in His written Word, in prayer and in any other ways that are particularly meaningful to you. In addition, you must live His prime directive; you must love; you must give of yourself. This doesn't have to be complicated. For example, a smile is an expression of love. It's a wonderful gift if the receiver, through your smile, can see God living within you. And if he can, then you are giving the greatest gift to your fellow man, through a simple smile, the gift of love.

Through our studying and learning about God, and through living His prime directive, we take on a tremendous armor that is impenetrable by the evil one. Thus by saying, "No!" to Satan in your greatest addiction, your greatest habitual sin, for forty days and nights, you develop a willpower stronger than you ever believed you could possess.

You'll replace the Satan within you with God within your very soul.

As you start your forty days to freedom, mark a calendar as "Day 1" and continue to mark it every day. Think each day about your progress, where you are on your path to freedom each day — one day at a time. And for each of these days you will say " "No!" "No!" to Satan! "No!" to evil! Evil cannot withstand God, and you have God and His strength within. You have willpower! You will be strong for just one day at a time. You will be constantly aware of your progress, the number of days you've accomplished, the number of days remaining. With each day you mark, you'll become more and more excited. Each day you will feel a new strength building within you, a new willpower — God's willpower.

Now it's time to start your forty-day journey in the desert of your soul. Begin each of your forty days with the reading, meditation and prayer provided. Read them often during each day, especially at times when you feel the need for God's strength. Add other readings or actions that may be especially meaningful to you; and always, always, throughout each of your forty days, radiate the love of Christ, the love of God. I recommend that you concentrate on resisting Satan in your greatest problem area for your first forty days. The procedure can be repeated over and over again in the future for other lesser problems. Remember God will be with you!

Day 1

Psalm 91:1-6

He who dwells in the shelter of the Most High will rest in the shadow of the Almighty.

I will say of the LORD, "He is my refuge and my fortress, my God, in whom I Trust."

Surely he will save you from the fowler's snare and from the deadly pestilence.

He will cover you with his feathers, and under his wings you will find refuge; his faithfulness will be your shield and rampart.

You will not fear the terror of night, nor the arrow that flies by day, nor the pestilence that stalks in the darkness, nor the plague that destroys at midday.

Meditation

Mark my calendar. This is the first day of my new beginning. For just this one day, I will not yield to the temptations of evil. I will remain strong, not on my own, for I have the strength of God with me. As I am confronted with temptation, I will loudly say, "No!" I will take notice of God's wondrous creation this day and appreciate it and love it. I will observe. I will love. I will give thanks for these amazing gifts. I will give honor and praise to He who is above all else and yet takes time to love and guide me as if I were the most important being in His magnificent creation.

72

Prayer

Our Father in heaven, hallowed be Your name, Your kingdom come, Your will be done on earth as it is in heaven.

Give us this day our daily bread and forgive us our trespasses as we forgive those who trespass against us.

And lead us not into temptation, but deliver us from the evil one.

For the kingdom, the power and the glory are Yours now and forever.

Amen.

Day 2

Psalm 91:14-16

"Because he loves me, " says the LORD, "I
will rescue him; I will protect him, for he
acknowledges my name.

He will call upon me, and I will answer
him; I will be with him in trouble, I will
deliver him and honor him.

With long life will I satisfy him and show
him my salvation."

<u>Meditation</u>

Mark my calendar. This is the second day of
my rebirth as a child of God. I know that today I
will face stronger temptation than yesterday. I must
hang tough just for today. I won't worry about
tomorrow, for if it comes, it is a gift from God. In
the gift of today I have great opportunity to serve
my God who created me wonderfully. He created
me to be free, and today I freely choose to serve
Him. Today His strength is with me, His love is
with me, and as I have faith in Him, He has faith in
me. My goal for this my second of forty days is
that when I lay my head on my pillow at the end of
this day, God will smile on me and say, "Well done,
my son (daughter)."

Prayer

Lord God, Creator of the heavens and this earth, thank You for revealing Yourself to me; and thank You for the gift of Your Son and His example of resisting the temptations of Satan for forty days. I pray that You will remain close with me this day and all the days of my life, my Lord, my God.

Day 3

Psalm 18:1-3

I love you, O LORD, my strength.

The LORD is my rock, my fortress and my deliverer; my God is my rock, in whom I take refuge.

He is my shield and the horn of my salvation, my stronghold.

I call to the LORD who is worthy of praise, and I am saved from my enemies.

Meditation

Mark my calendar. On this third day of my new beginning, I am encouraged. I have said "No!" for the past two days and have survived with the help and the strength of God. Though I know my temptation will be still stronger today, I now have reason and experience to believe I can make it. Though there are no other people in my desert, I am not alone; God is with me. Because of His strength within me, this third day I will continue to say "No!" in the face of Satan.

Prayer

My God, You have counted every hair on my head. Thank You for loving me so much that You have given me this miraculous way to overcome my harmful addiction. I believe, Lord, that You are all-powerful; and I ask that You empower me with Your strength and Your love this day so that together we may defeat Satan.

Day 4

Psalm 18:25-29

To the faithful you show yourself faithful, to the blameless you show yourself blameless, to the pure you show yourself pure, but to the crooked you show yourself shrewd.

You save the humble but bring low those whose eyes are haughty.

You, O Lord, keep my lamp burning; my God turns my darkness into light.

With your help I can advance against a troop; with my God I can scale a wall.

<u>Meditation</u>

Mark my calendar. This is the fourth day of my new beginning; and I can feel a change happening within me. There is a new strength, a new willpower that wasn't there before. I am a better person. I like myself and others more. The real me is coming to the surface. This is the strong, the loving, the good me who was repressed and now is being set free. I am becoming pleasing in the eyes of God. I can feel His strength growing within me. This day I will again say yes to love and no to Satan.

<u>Prayer</u>

Praise to You, my Lord, my Savior. You have seen fit to answer the prayer of one of Your creation who was trapped in a vice of sin and confusion. You have opened my eyes to the wonder of Your kingdom and majesty and power. I pray that I may dwell in Your house for all the days of my life.

Day 5

Psalm 18:16-19

He reached down from on high and took
    hold of me; he drew me out of deep
    waters.
He rescued me from my powerful enemy,
    from my foes, who were too strong for
    me.
They confronted me in the day of my
    disaster, but the LORD was my support.
He brought me out into a spacious place; he
    rescued me because he delighted in me.

Meditation

    Mark my calendar. This is day five of my forty days, and still I persist; my Lord persists. I will become a rock like Jesus is a rock. "My yoke is easy, and my burden is light, " He said (Matt. 11:30). Could it be He meant that with His strength within me, I can simply turn over control to Him and watch Him do His work? His work within me is truly beautiful. Perhaps someday I can help others to remove their heavy burdens and see their true beauty within. Together we persist. Together we continue our forty days.

Prayer

My Lord, I know You allowed my affliction for a purpose, which will result in good, for You are all good, all forgiving, all kind, all loving. Thank You for loving and protecting me. Thank You for these priceless gifts You are showering on me these forty days. Keep me strong in You my Lord, my God.

Day 6

Psalm 16:1-3

Keep me safe, O God, for in you I take
refuge.

I said to the LORD, "You are my Lord; apart
from you I have no good thing."

As for the saints who are in the land, they
are the glorious ones in whom is all my
delight.

Meditation

Mark my calendar. God is revealing new things
to me every day. My vision is changing, as I can
see God everywhere, in other people and
throughout His creation. The world is a beautiful
place filled with His glory. He is doing wonderful
things for me as these forty days continue. The
temptation is still there. Satan is still there, but I
have a new shield against him. With God's help,
my shield won't bend on this my sixth day.

Prayer

*Lord, words can never show my gratitude
for the new freedom You are granting to me. I
was blind to my bondage; but day by day, You
are setting me free. Please, Lord, be with me
and protect me all the days of my life; and
though I am not worthy, allow me to serve
You.*

Day 7

Psalm 16:7-8
I will praise the LORD, who counsels me;
    even at night my heart instructs me.
I have set the LORD always before me.
Because he is at my right hand, I will not be
    shaken.

Meditation

Mark my calendar. Strength and wisdom and peace are such wonderful gifts from God. I am learning that these are far above any material gifts. He has given me new vision, a more positive view of the world around me. I'm not blind to the problems that exist, but now I'm aware of opportunities for solutions that I never saw before. My temptation still exists, but somehow I feel the worst is behind. With God's help I will keep up my resistance, no matter what.

Prayer

Jesus, You have given me a great gift in the example of Your forty days in the desert. Help me to use Your gift wisely, not only to attain my own freedom of mind and spirit but also to help others attain the same freedom.

Day 8

Psalm 145:1-4

I will exalt you, my God the King; I will
   praise your name for ever and ever.

Every day I will praise you and extol your
   name for ever and ever.

Great is the LORD and most worthy of
   praise; his greatness no one can fathom.

One generation will commend your works
   to another; they will tell of your mighty
   acts.

Meditation

Mark my calendar. I am experiencing a miracle
just as surely as if I were back in time when Jesus
walked this earth. He has touched me with His
healing power through His example:

Jesus, full of the Holy Spirit, returned
from the Jordan and was led by the Spirit in
the desert, where for forty days he was
tempted by the devil. He ate nothing during
those days, and at the end of them he was
hungry.

The devil said to him, "If you are the Son
of God, tell this stone to become bread."

Jesus answerd, "It is written: 'Man does
not live on bread alone.'"

The devil led him up to a high place and
showed him in an instant all the kingdoms
of the world. And he said to him, "I will
give you all their authority and splendor,

for it has been given to me, and I can give it to anyone I want to. So if you worship me, it will all be yours."

Jesus answered, "It is written: 'Worship the Lord your God and serve him only.'"

The devil led him to Jerusalem and had him stand on the highest point of the temple. "If you are the Son of God, " he said, "throw yourself down from here. For it is written: 'He will command his angels concerning you to guard you carefully; they will lift you up in their hands, so that you will not strike your foot against a stone.'"

Jesus answered, "It says: 'Do not put the Lord your God to the test.'"

When the devil had finished all this tempting, he left him until an opportune time (Luke 4:1-13).

Prayer

Thank You, Jesus, for this wonderful tool — the example of Your forty days in the desert — that I may use to purge myself of the dominance of evil in my life. Thank You, Lord, for this expression of Your love for me.

Day 9

Psalm 145:17-18

The LORD is righteous in all his ways and
loving toward all he has made.
The LORD is near to all who call on him, to
all who call on him in truth.

Meditation

Mark my calendar. God is with me. For the past
eight days, He has been my fortress against Satan.
The temptation to sin continues; however, God's
strength in me is steadily growing. This new
willpower amazes me. Perhaps through Him, I will
become His rock. I would like that. That is my new
goal: to become a rock for my Lord.

Prayer

*O God, be with me closer now than ever
during my trial in the desert of my soul. Be my
rock and my strength that I may become Your
rock and Your servant. Help me, my Lord and
Savior, to learn more about You and the cause
of this new victorious happiness I feel.*

Day 10

Psalm 146:5-7

Blessed is he whose help is the God of
Jacob, whose hope is in the Lord his
God, the Maker of heaven and earth, the
sea, and everything in them — the Lord,
who remains faithful forever.

He upholds the cause of the oppressed and
gives food to the hungry. The Lord sets
prisoners free.

Meditation

Mark my calendar. My struggle continues, but
I feel I am winning. I have been here before, yet
this time is different. This time I am not alone. This
time God is with me. Why? Simply because I
asked Him to be. He was always there, just waiting
for my invitation. How fortunate I am to know Him
and to be loved by Him. Our journey continues on
this the tenth day.

Prayer

*O Lord, thank You for endeavoring to set
this prisoner free. I was a miserable wretch
until You entered my soul. Now I see value, for
I feel loved by You. You have lifted the
blinders from my eyes, and I see that I'm
wonderfully made in Your image. Be with me,
guide me, strengthen me this day and all the
days of my life. I ask this in the name of my
Lord and Savior, Jesus Christ.*

Day 11

Psalm 142:1-3
I cry aloud to the L ORD; I lift up my voice
    to the L ORD for mercy.
I pour out my complaint before him; before
    him I tell my trouble.
When my spirit grows faint within me, it is
    you who know my way.

<u>Meditation</u>

Mark my calendar. One-fourth of my journey is behind me. It seems longer than ten days. The first days were the longest and more filled with anguish. Now I am looking forward to the Lord's creation of each new day as an opportunity for victory over Satan. I know he will always confront me at some time during each day, but Jesus is my example. With God's help I continue to say, "No!" on this day eleven.

<u>Prayer</u>

Lord, thank You for the gifts You shower upon me. By answering my prayers, You show that You have forgiven my sins against You. I now pray that You will shower Your blessings on all those I have hurt in the past. Help me, Lord, to be aware that because all people are Your sons and daughters, they are my brothers and sisters. Help me always to look for You in others and to always treat all my brothers and sisters with love.

Day 12

Psalm 144:1-2
Praise be to the LORD my Rock, who trains
my hands for war, my fingers for battle.
He is my loving God and my fortress, my
stronghold and my deliverer, my shield,
in whom I take refuge.

Meditation

Mark my calendar. I am so happy that I started this journey, for I am becoming a new person. I am experiencing a rebirth of the whole purpose for my life. It's as if scales have been removed from my eyes and I'm seeing things clearly for the first time. I'm gaining control over my mind. I like the new me as my God and I together begin our twelfth day.

Prayer

Lord, You are my strength forever. I have been so blind in the past, refusing to see You even while I prayed to You. Help me never to forget Your healing power. Help me never to forget the way I was, blind and weak, not in control. Walk with me on this journey and all the journeys of my life.

Day 13

Psalm 13:1-4

The LORD is my shepherd, I shall not be in
want.

He makes me lie down in green pastures, he
leads me beside quiet waters, he restores
my soul.

He guides me in paths of righteousness for
his name's sake.

Even though I walk through the valley of
the shadow of death, I will fear no evil,
for you are with me; your rod and your
staff, they comfort me.

Meditation

Mark my calendar. Twelve days are behind me,
twelve days of resistance, love and strength. Of
what is ahead, only today is important. This day is
a gift from God with an opportunity to serve Him.
I will greet this thirteenth day with a smile on my
face and a song in my heart, a song of love for His
creation, a song of appreciation for His love and
faithfulness.

Prayer

*Lord, I love Your beauty and the place
where Your glory dwells. Thank You for the gift
of this new day and the opportunity to serve
You. I pray that I may be Your instrument of
love to others, and that I may see You in them,
and that they may see You in me.*

Day 14

Psalm 32:1-2

Blessed is he whose transgressions are
forgiven, whose sins are covered.

Blessed is the man whose sin the LORD
does not count against him and in whose
spirit is no deceit.

Meditation

Mark my calendar. How can it be that I have a
new beginning? I deserved punishment for my sins
of the past. I was ruled by Satan and though I was
deceived, yet the choice was mine. Now, looking
back, I see the choice was foolish. Yet rather than
punish me, God has forgiven me and suited me
with a new armor against the evil one, the armor of
faith. And in my hand, He has placed the sword of
love. He is teaching me that by having faith in Him
and by giving the love He gives me, I can achieve
more than winning all the wealth of the world.

Prayer

*Lord, I pray that You will remain close with
me through this day. Strengthen my faith in You
that I may serve You well and cause You to
smile. Help me to love and serve Your people.
Make my hands Your hands, my eyes Your eyes,
and my heart Your forgiving heart, so that Your
work on this earth may be done this day.*

Day 15

Psalm 32:5
Then I acknowledged my sin to you and did
  not cover up my iniquity.
I said, "I will confess my transgressions to
  the LORD" — and you forgave the guilt
  of my sin.

Meditation

Mark my calendar. Two weeks have passed
since God and I started on this journey in the desert
of my soul. My soul was barren then. It's still a
long way from a beautiful, fruitful garden, but
that's something I can now see as a possibility —
no, a probability. On this our fifteenth day, if it is
God's will, I will plant something beautiful in my
soul by serving Him.

Prayer

*Thank You, Lord, for being the gardener of
my soul. You are, one by one, throwing out the
weeds, then fertilizing, then planting Your
fruit. Thank You for opening my eyes and
showing me that the weeds and the fruit
cannot flourish together. If the weeds — my
sins — are not destroyed, then the fruit —
Your love in me — cannot blossom to its full
potential and multiply in others.*

Day 16

Psalm 18:30-33
As for God, his way is perfect; the word of
the LORD is flawless.
He is a shield for all who take refuge in
him.
For who is God beside the LORD?
And who is the Rock except our God?
It is God who arms me with strength and
makes my way perfect.
He makes my feet like the feet of a deer; he
enables me to stand on the heights.

Meditation

Mark my calendar. Jesus died that I might live
in and for Him. He no longer walks this earth
opening the minds and hearts of people, winning
their souls for His Father in heaven. Therefore, if
His work is to be done, if souls are to be saved, I
must do it. But before I do His work, I must purge
myself of Satan as Jesus did in His forty days or
instead I may set the wrong example and turn
people away from God. Jesus' sacrifice gives me
strength for this our sixteenth day.

Prayer

Jesus, I can see the nails holding Your feet and Your hands to that rough, splintery cross. The blood streaming down Your face is caused by thorns that dig into Your head from the crown fashioned by Your accusers. You look into Your mother's eyes and see her torment as she watches Your life slowly leave Your body. To breathe, You must push Your body up with Your feet, but the resulting pain from the nails is too great. You stop pushing, and again, hanging from Your hands, the pressure against Your chest suffocates You. You push up to breathe and repeat the painful cycle. Thank You, my Lord, for suffering this to set me free from my sins.

Day 17

Psalm 24:3-5
Who may ascend the hill of the LORD?
Who may stand in his holy place?
He who has clean hands and a pure heart,
    who does not lift up his soul to an idol or
    swear by what is false.
He will receive blessing from the LORD and
    vindication from God his Savior.

Meditation

Mark my calendar. The temptation of the evil one continues. It seems stronger now than a few days ago, but I must persevere. Too much has been won to turn back now. God is with me, and He wants to set me free. It would be so easy to give in to sin, but then I would be lost again, enslaved again, out of control again. No. Too much has been won. And I can feel God's strength surging within me on this day seventeen.

Prayer

Thank You, Lord, for answering my prayer. Thank You for coming to me in my hour of need and abiding with me. I love the way You make me feel: strong, positive, confident, focused. You give value and purpose to my life. I am amazed at Your work, my Lord, my God.

Day 18

Psalm 25:4-5
Show me your ways, O LORD, teach me
your paths; guide me in your truth and
teach me, for you are God my Savior,
and my hope is in you all day long.

Meditation

Mark my calendar. I can never repay the Lord
for all He has done for me. Only God himself can
defeat the cunning wiles of Satan. Only God can
forgive my sins and set me free from the prison
they create. Soon I will be free, really free, for the
first time in my life. I have been a prisoner for a
long time, but my God is setting me free for all
eternity.

Prayer

*My God, only You are the author of real
freedom. You are my liberator and my
champion, for I am not strong enough or
smart enough to defeat the wiles of Satan. I
will put my trust in You for all the days of my
life. Show me, Lord, the path of Your
righteousness and give me the strength to
follow Your way, the only way to happiness,
peace and fulfillment forever.*

Day 19

Psalm 25:8-10

Good and upright is the LORD; therefore he
instructs sinners in his ways.

He guides the humble in what is right and
teaches them his way.

All the ways of the LORD are loving and
faithful for those who keep the demands
of his covenant.

Meditation

Mark my calendar. My happiness is in my Lord.
In Him I find comfort during my journey. He alone
is always with me, always for me. He alone is
worthy of my trust, for He will never reject me,
never disown me. My inheritance is great with the
Lord; it is God Himself. After my journey, I will
know the joy of serving Him all the days of my life.

Prayer

*Lord, I pray that my desire for earthly
things be lessened and my desire for You be
increased. Help me to see Your ways clearly,
Lord; free my mind from all obstacles that
stand between us. Give me a new vision that I
may do Your will in all of life's challenges. Let
me focus on the goal of being with You in
heavenly bliss for all eternity.*

Day 20

Psalm 26:6-8

I wash my hands in innocence, and go about your altar, O LORD, proclaiming aloud your praise and telling of all your wonderful deeds. I love the house where you live, O LORD, the place where your glory dwells.

Meditation

Mark my calendar. God's creation is filled with beauty, and I am becoming one of His beautiful creations. His presence alone can change the impossible into the possible, into the probable, into the done. The ugly worm is becoming a beautiful butterfly because with Him I become strong and can overcome all ugliness. The battle is not yet over, but as long as God is with me, I can defeat Satan again on this twentieth day.

Prayer

Lord, be with me this day and remain strong in me for all the days of my life so that I may live for You. You are the only life for me, the song on my lips and in my heart. Foolish people store up wealth and seek the pleasures of the flesh; and they are deceived by the evil one. Keep my mind clear with Your presence, Lord, that I may continue to see the one true way to happiness, which is in You and through You.

Day 21

Psalm 27:1-3

The LORD is my light and my salvation —
whom shall I fear?

The LORD is the stronghold of my life — of
whom shall I be afraid?

When evil men advance against me to
devour my flesh,

When my enemies and my foes attack me,
they will stumble and fall.

Though an army besiege me, my heart will
not fear;

Though war break out against me, even
then will I be confident.

Meditation

Mark my calendar. This is war, good against
evil. I am the prize, my very soul. With God's help
I have the edge in this struggle, for He is the
Mightiest One, the All Powerful. But I must not
forget evil has trickery and defeat on its side. I
must remain alert to recognize my foe, for my loss
means the death of my soul, and winning means
eternal life in blissful glory with my God. I will
remain strong, and with faith as my shield and love
as my weapon, He and I will win this twenty-first
day.

Prayer

Lord, You are my rock, my salvation. With You I am everything; without You I am nothing. You have revealed Yourself and Your Son to me in my desert. You have answered my call for help. You have quenched my thirst with Your healing water. Though the shadow of death follows me on my journey, I will fear no evil, for You offer me eternal life.

Day 22

Psalm 27:4-5

One thing I ask of the LORD, this is what I seek: that I may dwell in the house of the LORD all the days of my life, to gaze upon the beauty of the LORD and to seek him in his temple. For in the day of trouble he will keep me safe in his dwelling; he will hide me in the shelter of his tabernacle and set me high upon a rock.

<u>Meditation</u>

Mark my calendar. God is good to me; He fills my heart with gladness. He allows me to conquer the challenges of each day and feel victorious, not because of my willpower and strength but because of His within me. I love feeling His presence; it is like no other feeling of being loved I have ever experienced. It must be a taste of heaven. As I endeavor to be His, He showers such wonderful gifts upon me: peace; contentment; happiness; other people to love, serve and forgive; daily opportunities to serve Him; and more. He is with me in all things on this twenty-second day in my desert.

<u>Prayer</u>

Thank You, Lord, for staying with me, for not giving up on me. I have faith, stronger than ever, that You will see me through this journey to its ultimate destination, the salvation of this soul. The victory is Yours, Lord; all praise and glory to You. You're the Mightiest One, the Holy One. Be the master of this newly won soul. This I ask in the name of my Lord and Savior, Jesus Christ, who lives and rules with You forever.

Day 23

Psalm 28:6-7

Praise be to the LORD, for he has heard my
cry for mercy.

The LORD is my strength and my shield; my
heart trusts in him, and I am helped.

My heart leaps for joy and I will give
thanks to him in song.

Meditation

Mark my calendar. God is doing great things
for me. He has set my foe behind me. I am no
longer the weak person I thought I was. The Lord
has given me a new vision to see through Satan, to
see through his lies, to recognize him in all his
disguises and trickery. My model now is Jesus; He
is my test of good or evil. When I am confronted
with a decision, I can simply ask what Jesus would
do. He is with me on this twenty-third day.

Prayer

*Lord, You are all powerful. You amaze me
with Your deeds, especially with Your love for
me. I thought I was unworthy, but You have
taught me of my importance to You, my God.
I am indeed fortunate to be so blessed. Help
me, Lord, to share this wonderful gift of
awareness of Your love with others. I was
blind, and now I see.*

Day 24

Psalm 30:1-3

I will exalt you, O LORD, for you lifted me
out of the depths and did not let my
enemies gloat over me.

O LORD my God, I called to you for help
and you healed me.

O LORD, you brought me up from the
grave; you spared me from going down
into the pit.

Meditation

Mark my calendar. The Lord gives me rest and
calm in this sea of turmoil, this sea of life. What a
treasure is the Lord, a treasure I hope to keep
forever, a mysterious treasure. I can only keep Him
by giving Him away to others, by sharing Him, by
telling others of what He has done for me. By
giving Him to others, I will receive Him more. Only
God can work in such mysterious and wonderful
ways as He is with me this day.

Prayer

Lord, thank You for giving Yourself to me, an undeserving sinner. In my human mind, I can never be worthy of You, my God, yet You see me as Your beautiful child, soiled and stained from my own foolishness and in need of Your loving, healing touch. I can never repay You for revealing these things to me; I can only sing praises to You all the days of my life. Praise and honor and glory to You Most Magnificent One, Ruler of the universe and Ruler of my soul.

Day 25

Psalm 30:11-12

You turned my wailing into dancing; you removed my sackcloth and clothed me with joy, that my heart may sing to you and not be silent.

O LORD my God, I will give you thanks forever.

Meditation

Mark my calendar. My Lord is so powerful. There is no foe that can stand against the power of His love for His creation. Yet I believe His greatest love is for the human soul; for He gives us the freedom to choose or reject Him. If we choose Him, He makes all things possible for us. His strength becomes our strength, against which evil cannot prevail on this our twenty-fifth day.

Prayer

Lord, You have opened my eyes to Your beauty and splendor. How blind I have been in ignoring You for earthly things. But You have been patient with me, Lord, and now I am changing, as the butterfly, into Your beautiful creation. I am reborn in You, my God, my Savior.

Day 26

Psalm 31:3-5
Since you are my rock and my fortress, for
the sake of your name lead and guide me,
Free me from the trap that is set for me, for
you are my refuge.
Into your hands I commit my spirit; redeem
me, O LORD, the God of truth.

Meditation

Mark my calendar. Through the Lord, a new sense of peace has come over me, as if I am being sheltered from the turbulence of the world. I believe this feeling to be the presence of the Holy Spirit Himself. Though I concentrate on today in resisting evil, I feel the power of the Holy Spirit within me will be victorious for all of the forty days. It is difficult to keep my heart from leaping with joy as He and I begin this twenty-sixth day in God's creation of a free soul.

Prayer

Praise to You, Almighty God, for Your power brings peace and contentment to this soul. You remake me according to Your will, and I am most pleased. No longer is my soul nothing more than a parched desert, trampled by the forces of evil. You, Lord, are planting a beautiful garden. You are watering and nourishing me with Your holy love. I am overwhelmed and grateful, my Lord, my God.

106

Day 27

Psalm 91:9-12

If you make the Most High your dwelling
— even the LORD, who is my refuge —
then no harm will befall you, no disaster
will come near your tent.

For he will command his angels concerning
you to guard you in all your ways; they
will lift you up in their hands, so that you
will not strike your foot against a stone.

Meditation

Mark my calendar. This is the day the Lord has made for me. I am His eyes, I am His ears, I am His feet, I am His hands and I am His voice in this world. I am the instrument with which my God goes about His work of winning souls away from the evil one. He has set me free to be His; how wondrous and great is the Lord. He resides with me and in me. He makes His home in me. I will love and serve the Lord on this twenty-seventh day.

Prayer

Praise to You, my God, for You are magnificent beyond all my understanding. I don't have to understand. It is enough to love and serve You all the days of my life. You are my God, the Source of my life. I thank You for this earthly life. I thank You for the opportunity to serve You. I thank You for setting me free and giving me a clear mind that I may see You and all your creation in all of its beauty and splendor.

Day 28

Psalm 92:1-5

It is good to praise the LORD and make music to your name, O Most High, to proclaim your love in the morning and your faithfulness at night, to the music of the ten-stringed lyre and the melody of the harp.

For you make me glad by your deeds, O LORD; I sing for joy at the works of your hands.

How great are your works, O LORD, how profound your thoughts.

Meditation

Mark my calendar. The Lord is my God and is becoming more my God every day as we drive Satan from my soul. God gives me a joy and peace in the solitude of this journey, which is something I have never before experienced. This truly is wonderful. This twenty-eighth day we begin in quiet strength.

Prayer

Lord, help me to never forget You, as Your people forgot You when they built and worshiped false idols after You saved them from the Egyptians. I ask that I may always remember and appreciate the miracle You are working in me. May I never forget the way I was before Your miracle, Lord. I was like a different person, a stranger, someone I didn't like. Protect and shield me, Lord, from the pursuit of Satan. Reside in me always. This I ask in the name of my Lord and Savior, Jesus Christ, who lives and reigns with You — one God, forever and ever.

Day 29

Psalm 31:21-22

Praise be to the LORD, for he showed his
wonderful love to me when I was in a
besieged city.

In my alarm I said, "I am cut off from your
sight!"

Yet you heard my cry for mercy when I
called to you for help.

Meditation

Mark my calendar. Here we are alone in the
desert of my soul. Yet I am not alone, for the Lord
is with me. Without His strength I wouldn't stand
a chance against the wiles of Satan. The Lord gives
me His strength and His discernment that I may be
strong and that I may identify Satan in all his subtle
disguises. For so long I was fooled. I passed off my
sins as simple human imperfections. I closed my
eyes to my slavery. I thought I was powerless to
change. Now the Lord is setting me free from my
bondage. He is opening a whole new life to me. He
is with me on this wonderful new day He has
made.

Prayer

Lord, how can I ever thank You for changing my life? Now I know the meaning of being reborn, as I am filled more and more each day with Your loving presence. You create a new life for me, a life of freedom, a freedom I have not known before these forty days. Abide with me this day and always.

Day 30

Psalm 32:8-10

I will instruct you and teach you in the way
   you should go; I will counsel you and
   watch over you.

Do not be like the horse or the mule, which
   have no understanding but must be
   controlled by bit and bridle or they will
   not come to you.

Many are the woes of the wicked, but the
   LORD'S unfailing love surrounds the man
   who trusts in him.

Meditation

Mark my calendar. "He who stands firm to the
end will be saved" (Matt. 24:13). Now I realize
that I can stay firm in my resistance against evil
because God is with me. On my own I could never
do this. The key is to ask for God's strength. That's
all! Just ask with a sincere heart, and it will be
given. God is wonderful. He is with me. He is
setting me free on this thirtieth day.

Prayer

*My God, you instill awe in me! Your deeds
are mighty and wonderful. Your enemies melt
away in front of you. Praise to You forever,
Lord of the heavens, King of my soul.*

Day 31

Psalm 34:1-3

I will extol the LORD at all times; his praise
will always be on my lips. My soul will
boast in the LORD; let the afflicted hear
and rejoice. Glorify the LORD with me; let
us exalt his name together.

Meditation

Mark my calendar. "The prayer of a righteous
man is powerful and effective" (James 5:16). God
has heard my prayer; He has answered. "And the
prayer offered in faith will make the sick person
well; the Lord will raise him up. If he has sinned,
he will be forgiven" (James 5:15). He heals me. He
forgives me. He reveals Himself to me. He shows
me His power. He shows me His compassion. The
instrument of His healing is His Son, Jesus. Thus
He expresses His great love for His Son and for
me. "God is love" (1 John 4:16).

Prayer

*How wonderful You are, Lord, that in all
the universe You pay attention to me. You
listen to my prayer. You grant my request for
Your healing guidance. Continue to show me
Your way, Lord, that I may serve Your cause.
Be with me in all my encounters this day.*

Day 32

Psalm 34:4-6

I sought the LORD, and he answered me; he
   delivered me from all my fears.

Those who look to him are radiant; their
   faces are never covered with shame.

This poor man called, and the LORD heard
   him; he saved him out of all his troubles.

Meditation

Mark my calendar. Though I know I must
concentrate on this day, the end is in sight. I feel a
burden has been lifted, and I am a new person. I
have been cured of my affliction. I have
experienced a miracle from the hand of my Lord.
But I will hold fast and complete the forty days in
the desert of my soul. Through this way — Jesus'
way — I will secure my transformation.

Prayer

*Lord, You have remained with me in battle.
You have comforted me in my misery. You
have given me willpower when I have been
confronted with Satan's temptation. You have
made me into a new person that I truly like.
Help me, Lord, to do Your will all the days of
my life. Be with me this thirty-second day.*

Day 33

Psalm 34:19-22

A righteous man may have many troubles,
but the LORD delivers him from them all;
he protects all his bones, not one of them
will be broken.

Evil will slay the wicked; the foes of the
righteous will be condemned.

The LORD redeems his servants; no one will
be condemned who takes refuge in him.

Meditation

Mark my calendar. The Lord is my strength and my refuge. With Him I can confront the evil one and not give in to temptation, which buries my soul. God has lead me out of the darkness into the light of His salvation. I will dwell in the house of my Lord all the days of my life. This is my choice as together we begin the thirty-third day in the desert of my soul.

Prayer

Lord, You are wonderful. You have opened my eyes and revealed the presence of the evil one so that I may resist him. You also reveal Yourself to me. How blind I have been in the past. I have missed so much of Your beauty. Surely I will love the Lord forever, for He has done great things for me.

Day 34

Psalm 36:5-7
Your love, O LORD, reaches to the heavens,
   your faithfulness to the skies.
Your righteousness is like the mighty
   mountains, your justice like the great
   deep.
O LORD, you preserve both man and beast.
How priceless is your unfailing love!
Both high and low among men find refuge
   in the shadow of your wings.

Meditation

   Mark my calendar. The Lord has helped me
through troubled times. He has tended my wounds.
He has provided an abundance of spiritual gifts. He
has seen to my physical needs. He cares for me
continuously. Why is this? I am a sinner. I am still
not perfect, but my Lord sees my heart is true. He
sees I want to shed the shackles of Satan and
become the servant of the Lord. He answers the
call of those who reach out to Him.

Prayer

   *Lord, You have revealed so much to Your
new servant. You have given me new sight that
I may see, where before I was blind. Your
goodness and kindness overwhelm me. You fill
my cup with Your love. You are the caretaker
of my soul, the Shepherd of my heart. You are
with me as we begin day thirty-four.*

117

Day 35

Psalm 36:8-10

They feast on the abundance of your house;
you give them drink from your river of
delights.

For with you is the fountain of life; in your
light we see light.

Continue your love to those who know you,
your righteousness to the upright in
heart.

Meditation

Mark my calendar. Here we are in what was once a barren desert, the desert of my soul. But now, as we approach the end of our journey, it is becoming a beautiful garden all because it has become the dwelling place of my Lord. I know this journey's end is just the beginning of a wonderful new life of serving my Lord and spreading His love. How wonderful is the Lord God. How fortunate I am, for He has saved me from the fiery furnace of my sin.

Prayer

Praise to You, Lord God, King of endless glory. You are magnificent above all, for with all Your power and might, You love Your children with a forgiving, caring heart. You give us the freedom to choose our own way, and when that way is the way of evil, You do not condemn us but patiently wait for us with open arms. You have given Your Son that we might find You. Be the Ruler of my heart, my soul and my mind on this thirty-fifth day.

Day 36

Psalm 37:1-4

Do not fret because of evil men or be envious of those who do wrong; for like the grass they will soon wither, like green plants they will soon die away.

Trust in the LORD and do good; dwell in the land and enjoy safe pasture.

Delight yourself in the LORD and he will give you the desires of your heart.

Meditation

Mark my calendar. I am made to do good, to serve God and to serve others. There is purpose in my life. I was not created to merely exist; what sense would that make? We are so blind. We believe "just getting by" or "get all you can get" describes life's fulfillment. No! Fulfillment is in serving, by loving, giving, forgiving and doing for the least of our brothers and sisters. This is the way of Jesus, the path He has laid for us to find our way back to Him, the Source of truth, the Way to eternal joy.

Prayer

Lord, Your beauty abounds throughout Your creation. As each day passes, You reveal more of Your beauty, more of Yourself to me. How may I serve You, my Lord? I eagerly await Your instructions. You have taught me that by serving You I express my love for You. You are the object of my desire. To be with You for all eternity is my greatest wish.

Day 37

Psalm 40:4-5

Blessed is the man who makes the LORD his trust, who does not look to the proud, to those who turn aside to false gods. Many, O LORD my God, are the wonders you have done.

Meditation

Mark my calendar. God is good to me. His blessings shine like the sun before me. He has cured my affliction and frustrated my enemy, the evil one. How can I ever repay the Lord for all He has done for me. I will start by being His and being open to His command. His work is not difficult but joyful, helpful and productive. I will watch and listen for His message this day thirty-seven.

Prayer

Lord, You are all good and all powerful. You cure the incurable. Help me to be the instrument of Your love on this earth. Help me to reflect Your love and goodness to others who are all my brothers and sisters. I am Yours, Lord, to do with as You please.

Day 38

Psalm 42:7-8

Deep calls to deep in the roar of your waterfalls; all your waves and breakers have swept over me.

By day the LORD directs his love, at night his song is with me — a prayer to the God of my life.

Meditation

Mark my calendar. I have journeyed a long way with the Lord my God, and He has been faithful to me. He has stood by me, as He did with His son, through all the temptations of Satan. I, too, am His child. Wonderful and powerful is the Lord in what He can achieve through His people. That's the key—to be His, to simply surrender to His love. Then all things are possible.

Prayer

You, O Lord, are my God, my strength. In all the universe there is nothing that can withstand You. You have created a miracle in this mere mortal's life. You have changed mortal to immortal; for Your greatest desire is to have your children freely choose to reside with You in eternity. Thank You for loving me, Lord. Continue Your love on this day and all the days of my life. Allow me to serve You this day.

Day 39

Psalm 43:3-4

Send forth your light and your truth, let them guide me; let them bring me to your holy mountain, to the place where you dwell.

Then I will go to the altar of God, to God, my joy and my delight.

Mediation

Mark my calendar. The Lord guides me in His ways. As I accept His guidance and try my best to live His way, He protects me and showers me with His blessings. He leads me to other people like me who are trying to live His way and serve Him. He blesses me every moment of my life in all things I do. What a wonderful discovery is the way of the Lord.

Prayer

Praise be to You, my Lord, my God. Your loving hand guides all Your creation. Only misguided people disrupt Your flow. Bring them into Your fold, Lord. Help Your servants to bring them into Your fold that they, too, may know the joy of living in Your light and being guided in all things by Your gentle and loving hand.

Day 40

Psalm 52:8-9

But I am like an olive tree flourishing in the
house of God; I trust in God's unfailing
love for ever and ever.

I will praise you forever for what you have
done; in your name I will hope, for your
name is good.

I will praise you in the presence of your
saints.

Meditation

Mark my calendar. This is the last day in the
desert of my soul, the last day in my confrontation
against Satan. But now my greatest weakness is
turned to power, for my God has overcome that
which was against Him and has created a new
disciple, a new rock. I am that disciple! I am that
rock! God has revealed Himself and His Son to me
in my healing. He has removed my demon. Great
is the name of the Lord! I will love and serve Him
all the days of my life.

Prayer

All praise to You, my Lord, my God, for You have set me free! I am freed from my bondage to Satan and his temptation. How wonderful is this freedom, how joyous, a taste of heaven. I am made anew; I am reborn in the Lord. Here is true wealth, true happiness, true fulfillment. All praise to You, my Lord, my God. Help me spread Your miraculous healing to Your people in need. Give me the courage to give witness to Your work in me.

Praise God, we are free! It seems as if for the first time in our life, we are truly free. Our mind is no longer a slave to the contemplation of evil thoughts and actions. Our mind is clear. It's as if we've had a cancer surgically removed. When we look back at our past thoughts and actions, we are amazed at how far we had fallen. But now we are back. The prodigal child has returned. The incurable has been cured. How is this possible? There can only be one answer: God's unquenchable love for us. Praise God! Never forget! Never forget how we were. Never forget who cured us.

Now you can concentrate better on your work. Your performance has improved. You see other people differently, as fellow creations of God. You look for and find God within others. You act with true love, true charity. You see the whole world from a different perspective. You are at peace with yourself and with God. You realize that with God all things are possible; nothing is impossible. You are happy, truly happy. You realize the only Source of happiness, the only Source of peace, the only Source of freedom is God, His strength and His love that now lives within you.

This doesn't mean you can relax after the forty days. Satan will never quit in his quest to own your soul. At the same time, God will never force you to choose His way. We can see this in the Israelites, who built and worshiped golden images after God freed them from the Egyptians. In the same way, America, after being founded on principles of freedom, justice and godliness, has turned its back on morality and God. Once we are free from our enslavement, addiction or obsession, like the Israelites we can choose to chase another false god. For example, you may have been cured of sexual addiction, and now you realize with your new freedom and ability to concentrate, you can better pursue financial wealth. If you fall into this trap, you will become enslaved again with a different addiction.

You must keep your guard up. How? By praying and staying in communication with God. The more His love fills your heart and your mind, the stronger you are in resisting Satan. You create a positive, God-within momentum. Pray for faith; pray for knowledge of Him; pray for His love; pray to be used in His service. By believing in Him, you will overcome all fear of this world. By knowing Him, your mind will experience the greatest wonders of the universe. By being filled with His love, His Holy Spirit, you will experience the presence of God Himself dwelling within you. And by serving Him, by sharing His love, which demands to be shared, you give the greatest service to humanity and to God. For by loving others, you are doing as God wishes you to do and, therefore, returning His love to Him in a nourishing, growing way. You become a mirror of God, a son or daughter of God, and ultimately one with God in immortality in a blissful existence beyond all human understanding or contemplation.

By successfully coming through the forty-day

desert of your soul, you ended your enslavement to sin. You became truly free—free to see the world from a different perspective, perhaps for the first time. Your mind is no longer ruled by what is socially acceptable because you can now see society for what it is, misled and corrupt. And now, with this new clarity of mind, if you open your mind you will find the one way, the one truth, the one life, the life with God. You will recognize all the false gods and all the tricks of Satan who will still try to lead you astray and enslave you. But you have a new measuring stick—God. All that is not of Him is false and a lie.

With your new clarity of mind, you become aware that some who say they are of God are liars. You have a new power of discernment that can see Satan behind their lies. Your clarity of mind will enrich every aspect of your life. The people in your life become more valuable to you, and you treat them with love. You're more aware of their feelings, and you have a new desire to make others happy instead of just seeking happiness for yourself.

No matter how good your spiritual life was before your forty days, you now have a new awareness of God and His role in your life. You become aware of the new freedom He has given you, the freedom to choose Him. He will never force Himself on you. This is contrary to the tactics of Satan, who will use every trick to enslave you. Instead, God offers you the free choice to possess Him rather than be possessed by Him. He offers

Himself freely to you in so many ways, primarily in His love. He gave His Son to you in the greatest sacrifice, the greatest act of love in human history. Jesus was born to die a humiliating, painful death so that people would turn from their sinful ways and follow God's way to eternal life with Him.

And now you have the key to the gates of heaven. Your prime directive, the reason for your existence on this earth, is to love others as God loves you, unselfishly giving of yourself to the people in your life. You have purged yourself of the evil one, and you can now say the choice of your path for the rest of your life is yours to make.

O, Lord, thank You for the gift of Your forty days in the desert. Thank You for purging Satan from my soul and allowing me to experience the miraculous cleansing and freedom of mind and spirit as was experienced by Your Son, my Lord and Savior, Jesus Christ.

Forty Days in Your Desert

Chapter 7

A NEW YOU

I'm a salesman by occupation. Sales is a result-oriented profession, as are most occupations. It seems all of us are more interested in what we achieve rather than how we get it. So let's indulge ourselves for a minute and look at the results of your forty days. Let's start with the personal results. First, you are free! Oh sure, Satan is still trying to tempt you with that old hang-up. He will never stop trying to enslave you. But you— my friend, my brother, my sister — are a new person, and the newest thing about you is your new inner strength—a strength that laughs at Satan and causes God to smile and say to you, "My child!"

This new, strong person has the ability to function better in this world. You are able to think with a clear mind; and you see the world through different eyes. You now see hope, not only for yourself but for others, for the whole world. You have realized the fruits of your hope and faith, for without faith in God, in Jesus and in yourself, you would not have attempted the forty days. Now that you have experienced personal proof of the reality of God and Jesus, now that you have experienced the power and the truth of the forty-day method He gave you, you realize it's all true. All His teachings are true. You realize your life doesn't end when your body dies. You realize that ahead of you is a glorious life in eternity with God. You also realize God has put you on this earth for a purpose, and now more than ever you must endeavor to fulfill that purpose, being thankful to God for healing your affliction.

There may be a tendency here for you to be overzealous, not in God's eyes but in the eyes of others. Since we are here not to alienate people from God but to win them to Him, be aware of their feelings and reactions to you. Let them see a better you, not a fanatic. Let them see a person they want to emulate. Draw them, attract them to God. How? Simply with your love. Be kind, be good, be helpful and be charitable, be happy—because you are happy in your new freedom, happy that such a burden has been lifted. Share that happiness, and help others to lift their burdens. They, too, have addictions, obsessions, guilt, pain and the miserable feeling of being lost. You can be their "good shepherd." You can bring them back to God's flock with your love.

Why do we want to be constantly on the alert for opportunities to give, spread and multiply God's love? Because God is counting on us. Those of us who are fortunate enough to have heard the message have an obligation to become agents for God. Jesus no longer walks this earth. Until His return, we are the instruments God is relying upon to do His work. But why bother? Wouldn't it be simpler to let someone else do all the work? Aren't there plenty of enthusiastic people to convert the world?

Until Satan has been defeated and eliminated from the face of the earth, we all are needed. Just because we think anything can be preferred to doing God's work, we can assume Satan is still influencing us in a subversive way, tempting us to concentrate on anything other than spreading God's love. We simply can't outgive God. As much love as we give, we will receive back much more from God. This love is the one treasure we are able to take with us into the next life, though this is not our motivation. Our motivation must be to open the eyes of others so they may see what we have seen, the path to salvation. We sincerely want to save souls. We sincerely want everyone to feel the peace, the harmony, the ecstasy of living with God.

There may be a second healthy motivation for our wanting to do God's work: our love for Him. He has saved us from condemning ourselves to hell; and we are grateful. We know there is no way we can ever repay the miracle of our healing, but because of it, we feel compelled to serve Him, and by serving Him to love Him for the rest of our days.

Now we become opportunists for God. He will provide the opportunities for us to display our love. Just remain always open, always mindful, always prayerful, asking Him to open the doors to the path He wants you to travel. We often have a choice between His path and the path of the world. Sometimes the path of the world is disguised to look like God's path. Pray for the gift of discernment and put the opportunity to the test of serving God, of spreading His love. Many causes that seem to be for humanity are just methods to manipulate the many to serve the few. Nazism and communism are examples.

Any movement that claims a man or a woman as its leader may possibly be humanistic in its intent, but it will fail without the leadership of God. Be wary of any organization that presents its leader as Godlike. The closer to God the leader becomes, the more he should become the servant acknowledging God as the true leader, the true inspiration. But if he jealously clings to his position of leadership, then he is self-serving and rejecting God's way.

God's cause doesn't promise physical food or jobs or equality on earth for everyone. God has told us the poor will always be with us. Therefore, we know that poverty, while providing an opportunity for us to serve others and God, will never be eradicated while Satan rules the earth. We will always find someone materially better off than we are. If our reach is for equality by man's definition, we are doomed to frustration. Physical and material conquests are all meaningless and empty without love, for love is the ultimate achievement. Just as Jesus is love incarnate, our path should lead us to become more like Jesus, striving also to become love incarnate. Is this possible? Do we know anyone who is a living example of love? If not, perhaps it's time we opened our eyes to our surroundings. Such people do exist. They're the ones who astonish us by smiling at adversity as simply another opportunity for giving love. These are people we should want to know and emulate.

After our forty days in the desert, we must actively stay close to God because Satan never rests. He will continue to pursue us. If we continue to possess God in our hearts and souls, we can laugh at Satan when we experience his temptations. We must continue to pray for others and for ourselves. God wants to help us every step of our way for the rest of our life. Be aware He is with us even in the smallest things. Nothing is too trivial for our petition. Start every day asking Him to be with you, to guide you, to give you His strength, to give you the strength of Jesus. Look for Him in others, share Him, give Him, give of yourself.

Hunger and thirst for knowledge of God. Become a reader of books that will add to your spiritual growth such as the writings of Thomas Merton. I suggest you start with a good study Bible, such as the *Serendipity Bible for Groups*. If you can study in a small group of two or more, you will learn faster and in a more meaningful way. Start with the four Gospels of the New Testament. Then you can go back in time to the Old Testament and more easily see how it foretold Jesus' coming and then forward in time to the remainder of the New Testament to experience the development of the early Christian church.

Two prerequisites are necessary for gaining knowledge of God. First, we must want to know about Him for the proper reason, such as our love for Him or our desire to serve or emulate Him. Second, we must allow God to teach us according to His schedule with His tools, of which the Bible is only one. Other learning tools may be our experiences with other people or, actually, anything in His creation. Be aware of God; be constantly listening to receive His message. He may withhold knowledge from you because He is not ready to reveal it, or may feel you are not ready to receive it. That must be all right with us. After all, He's God. It's not necessary that we know everything; otherwise, what's faith for? He may impart knowledge to you on a need-to-know basis. Be aware that it can come at any time and anywhere. An idea may pop into your mind seemingly out of nowhere (He allows nothing to happen without purpose). You may be in a group discussion when you give an answer you didn't previously know, and somehow you know it's the right answer.

If He imparts knowledge of Himself to you, He has a purpose. It may relate to the special service He wants from you. Hunger to serve Him. Be certain, He has something very special for every one of us to do. Pray for direction, and be aware the answers may come when you least expect them and may not always be the answers you want. Be open to His will over yours. This openness can only be the act of a free person without hang-ups or enslavement to Satan. God may wait until you have won such freedom before revealing His plan for you, as was true with the author.

After your forty days, you'll find yourself changed, the same person but better. You'll find yourself easier to like, easier to love because now you are free to radiate love. A burden will have been lifted from your mind, from your inner being, from the real you. As a result, you have experienced a conversion. You realize that this was only possible through God and that you have tapped the ultimate power in the universe. You have experienced a miracle as the slavery of your mind has ended. You are in control for the first time in a long, long time.

Regardless of your conscious beliefs before your conversion, you now know that God exists. Only through Him was your healing possible. You have a new faith, and you are grateful. You see, this is the person you always wanted to be. This chapter is for the new you, the you who has a new lease on life, the you who was lost and now is found, the you who has a new family, the family of God. Welcome, my brother, my sister!

You now feel indebted to God. This is not a burdensome type of debt; rather you feel compelled to take action. You want to make God first in your life, but you don't know how. Start with prayer and express to God that you want Him to be first in your life and you'll initiate some effort that will strengthen your union with Him. This could be church attendance, regular Bible study or volunteering for charitable work. The action must be meaningful to you and frequent. The greater the frequency the better. The more God fills your life, the less chance Satan has of reentering it. Next — and this is very important — ask God to open the doors He wants you to enter. If you ask Him to give your life new direction, He will. If you now realize He has saved a life that you thought had little value, which was only being lived for itself, you must also realize now He has a purpose for you. God doesn't create waste. He creates bounty, and He wants you to be bountiful. Isn't that wonderful? You have great value. There is a great reason for your existence. You are a great person, and if you ask God to reveal your path to greatness, which is the reason for your creation, **He will!** Realize we're speaking here of greatness not in men's eyes but in God's eyes. If because of God men esteem you highly, accept it with humility and give the credit to God.

Now a second miracle has happened. First, you have been saved from an empty life, a life of enslavement to greed or lust or some other aspect of misdirected self-fulfillment. You are free! Free to choose your way to live the rest of your life. Free to choose God's way; and this truly is a free choice. He will never force Himself on you as Satan does. And this is where the second miracle occurs; this is your spiritual rebirth, a true rebirth in your whole way of thinking, in your whole way of living. Now the clouds have been lifted from your mind, and you clearly see the way to true happiness for the first time. You used to think only religious fanatics were wrapped up in God all the time, but what you have experienced is not religion, for it can be experienced regardless of which religion you profess or whether or not you are a member of any organized religion. In fact, since and because of your rebirth, you can identify the false fanatics and the false religions. Any religion that professes anything but love for any of God's creation is false. No, you haven't experienced religion. You have experienced rebirth, the beginning of a close personal relationship with your Creator. Now you can use religion to nurture that relationship because the right religion will help you to unite with others in spreading God's love.

Oh, Lord, thank You for setting me free. Help me to radiate love to everyone You allow me to meet. Open the doors to opportunities to serve You. I want to make You first in my life. I'll start by _____.

Chapter 8

TAP THE GREATEST POWER

God's measure of man is entirely different from man's measure of man. Man is result-oriented. What have we produced? How much have we made? How much have we accumulated? We all tend to look back at our lives. If the results aren't there or they're insufficient in our judgment, we're disappointed or dissatisfied. We use our peers, people with similar backgrounds and circumstances, as our gauge. If they outperform us, if they have bigger homes, more expensive cars or more money in the bank, we see ourselves as inferior. This is the stuff of which a mid-life crisis, an all-too-common malady in our society, is made. Ridiculous, isn't it?

Sons and daughters of God, do not spend your time in worry, but choose to spend your time in the joy of the practice of Jesus' commandments. He gave us three: love God, love our neighbors and love ourselves. These three He ultimately summarized and combined into one: love each other. For when we love each other, we are expressing the ultimate act of love for God because we are doing His work on earth. And when we love each other, we are expressing the ultimate act of love for ourselves in the gift of eternal life with God. This gift is ours to give to ourselves. How? By following, by living Jesus' command. This gift cannot be given; it is a free choice for each one of us; and the only way to obtain the gift is through living Jesus' command, a life of giving love to all we touch, to all we see, to all we experience, unselfishly, not to attain the gift but simply because it is the will of God who is our true Father.

The only way to the Father is through Jesus, through following His command. We know this is so not only because of His teachings but also because of His resurrection. If His resurrection is a lie, then Jesus' teachings and commandments are lies. Since we know in our hearts after we're exposed to His teachings that His teachings are the ultimate truth, then it follows that His resurrection also must be true as part of His teachings. One is incomplete without the other. To say His resurrection is not true is to say that God is incomplete or imperfect. Again, we know in our heart of hearts, which is our God-given power of discernment, that God is the one perfect being.

But there are those who demand physical proof. Probably for them no amount of proof would be enough because ultimately God requires faith and trust from us. As a token of love for us, God gave us physical proof of His Son's existence, His life, His death and His resurrection. This physical proof is a photograph taken at the exact instant of Jesus' resurrection. The photograph is known as the Shroud of Turin. Many tests have been conducted on this holy cloth, most conclusive, some inconclusive. For the "doubting Thomases," try to explain how this image of the scarred, battered body of Jesus could have been manufactured by mortals, even with today's technology, two thousand years ago. Also consider the timing of the creation of the image, since it was created by the burst of energy and light from the resurrection of Jesus at the most important moment in the history of mankind. Thereby, the Shroud of Turin is physical evidence not only of Jesus' regaining life but also of the truth of His teachings (New Testament) and the teachings of those who foretold His coming.

There are several books on the Shroud if you should care to study this fascinating subject. To say

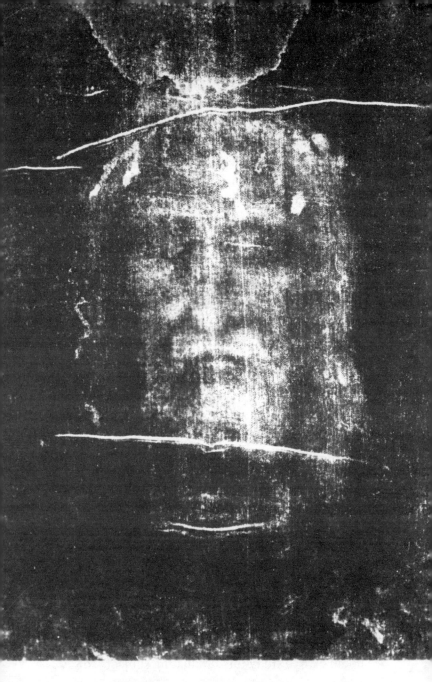

The Face of Our Lord Jesus Christ as revealed
by photography from the Holy Shroud

the reality of the Shroud is impossible is to limit God whose limitless power is beyond all human understanding or contemplation. After study, I have accepted on faith that the Shroud of Turin is the burial cloth of Jesus because I accepted, also on faith, Jesus as the Son of God. Logic simply confirms my belief, first in Jesus, since through study of His word I find Him to be both love and truth incarnate. Second, with my faith in Jesus, I find a visual recording of His resurrection totally logical as a simple remembrance of the occasion for the "doubting Thomases," as Jesus did express concern for my namesake in His gospel.

Our life on this earth is like a single tick on the clock in the continuum of time, and we get all caught up in the gluttony of materialism, which can't last beyond this moment. Americans have become famous for their short-term perspective. Does this way of life make us happy? What is happy? We ask, "Where will I be five years from now?" If at the end of the five years we haven't achieved or accumulated enough, we're failures. What if we did achieve our goal? Are we happy? Or empty? And we really don't understand why. What is really important? What is the treasure we can take with us for all eternity? How does God measure us? How should we measure ourselves?

If all our material accomplishments are meaningless to God, which we know to be true, what is important to Him? How does He measure us? Actually, He's quite easy on us. All He cares about is how we treat one another. Not how much we get but how much we give, of ourselves, of His gifts to us, to others, to His children. We are all His children, and just as any proud parent, He wants the best for us. But the best is not in this fleeting lifetime. The best is in eternity with Him. Similarly, for those who are parents, we need to realize for each child there exists three parents; for without God as a parent there is no spark of life and humanity, which is His presence at conception. We also need to realize that wanting the best for our children is wanting them to be loving, caring, generous people so they will one day be reunited with us, all three parents, in eternal bliss.

There is a great mystery here that most people don't take the time to see. The long-term perspective and the short-term perspective are one. The action we take now is what is important to God, and that is how He measures our entire lives. Every day we have contact with other people face-to-face, perhaps by telephone, certainly in our thoughts. Every day is loaded with opportunities to serve Him by serving others. These others are all our brothers and sisters, as we all have the same heavenly Father. He sees no class distinctions, no differences in quality among His children. How can we profess to love God if we don't love all of His children and all of His creation? Every time we abuse in thought or action any of His creation, we abuse Him. This is not an expression of love. What good is accomplished by attending church services where we are expressing love for God if we are not living that love in every moment of our lives? How do we start? Start by treating everybody just a little bit better than we ordinarily would, making sure we're genuine and unselfish. Though we're doing this to please God, we will experience newness, and others will see us as a new person. We'll like the results.

A second great mystery lies in the fact that it is never too late to change, but change we must; the sooner we change, the greater our rewards in this life before joining God in heaven. Through this change or conversion to His way rather than our way, we choose to be with Him for all eternity. If we are stubborn children and choose the way of man, the way of the world, the way of materialism, the way of get, not give, then we choose against God's way. We choose not to be with Him. We reject Him, and we choose the hell of being without Him.

It has been said, "Knowledge is power." Certainly this is true, for the better informed we are before we attempt any endeavor, the greater our chance for success. But is knowledge the ultimate power, or politics, or brute strength, or wealth? All of these have been possessed and applied down through the ages, and all have ultimately been defeated. No power has proved invincible save one — love! All other sources of power have been defeated by love. Love alone reigns invincible, undefeated, even in contest with the power of death. Understand, however, it reaches perfection, not through having but through giving. In the act of giving love, we break down all barriers, we conquer and consume all opposition for God, for good, for freedom, for happiness.

I am involved in a movement to bring Christ into the prisons throughout our land. It has been one of the most spiritually rewarding things I have ever done. "Whatever you did for one of the least of these brothers of mine, you did for me" (Matt. 25:40). Through this dynamic ministry, Satan is being defeated in places that he once dominated. For information, contact Kairos Inc., 140 N. Orlando Ave., Suite 220, Winter Park, FL, 32789-3680; phone (407) 629-4948.

The action that interests God is love. If we always act out of love — love for God, love for His other children and love for ourselves — then we are acting in accordance with His way. The results of our loving others in thought and action will reward us richly in how we feel about ourselves. We'll be filled with a wonderful sense of peace and contentment. We'll feel the presence of God working in and through us, and we'll experience a sense of harmony with the universe. All fear of the unknown future will vanish, for we know our future is with Him, and we are confident of His love for us as we feel it growing every day. We'll also see those we are loving change for the better. We are tapping into, living and applying the greatest power in existence, the power of love. Nothing can withstand it. It must create good, and though we will see much good come from our love, seeing what we achieve really doesn't matter. The achievements we can leave to God. His yardstick or measure of success is easy. It is simply that we love.

He doesn't demand that we accept His way in blind faith. He'll allow us to test the water. All we have to do is try His way, His method of living, to realize this is the only way of achieving true happiness. And in the trying, in the testing, in the proving, He also proves His existence to us in the truth of His way and in the very real experience of His presence in our lives.

A final note of caution: Be aware that people who are close to you may talk more against your devotion to God than they did against your past sins. They may relate more to your sins because they too are sinners whether they admit it or not. Those of us who are trying to live according to God's law are rare. We will be condemned as fanatics by those who are lost, even those who are close to us, even our own flesh and blood. This doesn't mean our loved ones are bad people, but they are misguided if their thoughts and actions are ruled by society instead of by God. Our devotion may threaten them if they think they would have to sacrifice too much to be like us. In reality, all they would sacrifice is their bondage to sin, thereby attaining true freedom, perhaps for the first time in their lives. Those close to us also will have trouble accepting our transformation as genuine. They knew us as we were. Even Jesus had problems with this in His hometown.

We suffer when our loved ones ridicule us. We try to influence them to change their ways because we want for them the same happiness and freedom we have found, but they often condemn us more. If we truly love them as God loves us, we'll realize we may be their only chance for eternal bliss. Take heart, stand strong in your faith, for you will not go back no matter what the cost. Remember your bondage. Satan would like to have you back, but stand firm in your resolve. Once you have tasted this freedom, you can never go back to your old ways.

Pray for your loved ones who are now alienated from you. Don't preach to them; don't argue with them; instead, set an example. Continue to use Jesus as your role model. Perhaps with time, they will see your conversion as genuine. Perhaps with time, they will see something desirable in you which they lack. Perhaps with time, you will become their role model.

You will grow from this experience. Every time you do battle with Satan and win, you become stronger and more committed to God's way. Be aware of your continuing transformation and be happy with it. You'll feel as if you're being molded by God for some special purpose, and you are! He does have a special purpose for you, one that is unique to you in His service. Rejoice, hold firm to your course and have faith that He will reveal your calling. Never underestimate Satan, for he will try to derail you. Your best defense is to stay close to God by doing His works, by associating with people who are walking your path, by praying, by being an active and enthusiastic member of your church, and by never forgetting the awesome gifts God has showered on you, especially your forty days to freedom.

My Lord, my God, thank You for loving me and for setting me free from the slavery of my sins. Help me to remain strong in You by being ever-present with me in my thoughts and actions. Never let me forget that You are the way, the truth, the life and the power over all the universe; for You, my Lord, are Love.

Epilogue

I hope this message has been the instrument of a wonderful transformation in your life, a transformation that has truly set you free from bondage to your worst demon or obsession. I pray this book will continue to benefit you on your walk to a blissful eternity.

You will meet others who will be candidates for the *Forty Days to Freedom* miracle procedure.

Epilogue

Additional books may be obtained either through your local bookstore or by mailing ~~$7.00 per copy~~ to Freedom Ministries, Inc., 1855 W. State Road 434, Suite 250, Longwood, Florida 32750-5071. ~~Order ten or more for $6.00 per book or forty or more for $5.00 per book.~~

If you would like to join Freedom Ministries, Inc. in our goal of making this message available to all souls-in-need throughout the world, we will ask three things of you:

1. A written testimonial of how *Forty Days to Freedom* enriched your life,
2. Your prayers for the success of our mission,
3. Your financial support (tax deductible).

As stated earlier, Jesus no longer walks this earth working His miracles and spreading knowledge about His Father. If His work is to be continued, it must be done by His followers. This is more necessary today than ever before as people find themselves helpless against the wiles of Satan; and society more and more turns its back on God. Help us to help them to take on the strength of Jesus so Satan's influence can be eradicated in their lives and eventually in all of society. We will keep our benefactors informed of their progress in this blessed task.

Again, I hope this message has enriched your life beyond all anticipation and that you will remain God's rock and His messenger and, most of all, His expression of love for all the days of your life.